SPEAK THUS

# Speak Thus

CHRISTIAN LANGUAGE IN CHURCH AND WORLD

Craig Hovey

CASCADE Books • Eugene, Oregon

SPEAK THUS
Christian Language in Church and World

Copyright © 2008 Craig Hovey. All rights reserved. Except for brief quotations in critical publications or reviews, no part of this book may be reproduced in any manner without prior written permission from the publisher. Write: Permissions, Wipf and Stock Publishers, 199 W. 8th Ave., Suite 3, Eugene, OR 97401.

Cascade Books
A Division of Wipf and Stock Publishers
199 W. 8th Ave., Suite 3
Eugene, OR 97401

www.wipfandstock.com

ISBN 13: 978-1-55635-504-2

*Cataloging-in-Publication data:*

Hovey, Craig, 1974–

    Speak thus : Christian language in church and world / Craig Hovey.

    xxiv + 146 p. ; 23 cm.

    ISBN 13: 978-1-55635-504-2

    1. Theology. 2. Christian ethics. I. Title.

BR121.2 .H68 2008

Manufactured in the U.S.A.

Revised Standard Version of the Bible, copyright 1952 [2nd edition, 1971] by the Division of Christian Education of the National Council of the Churches of Christ in the United States of America. Used by permission. All rights reserved.

*To my teachers*

CONTENTS

*Acknowledgements* ix
*Preface* xi
*Introduction* xiii

NEGOTIATING

1 Narrative Proclamation and Gospel Truthfulness  3
2 On Hauerwas and Yoder  18
3 Democracy Beyond Democracy  39

SPEAKING

4 Metaphors We Die By  47
5 Story and Eucharist  66
6 Forester, *Bricoleur*, and Country Bumpkin  84
7 This Is My Brother's World  100

PROCLAIMING

8 How Free Are We?  123
9 Basking and Speaking in Ordinary Time  129

*Bibliography* 135
*Index* 141

ACKNOWLEDGEMENTS

Earlier versions of some of the chapters have appeared as follows. They appear here, in some cases, with significant modifications: "Narrative Proclamation and Gospel Truthfulness: Why Christian Testimony Needs Speakers" (chapter 1) will also appear in a forthcoming title by Herald Press on Radical Orthodoxy and the radical Reformation, edited by Chris Huebner and Tripp York. "The Public Ethics of Stanley Hauerwas and John Howard Yoder: Difference or Disagreement?" (chapter 2) has appeared in *A Mind Patient and Untamed: Assessing John Howard Yoder's Contribution to Theology, Ethics, and Peacemaking*, edited by Ben C. Ollenburger and Gayle Gerber Koontz (Telford, PA: Cascadia, 2004). Copyright © 2004 by Cascadia Publishing House. Used by permission, all rights reserved. "Democracy Beyond Democracy" (chapter 3) appeared in *Theology Today* 61 (2004) 355–59. "Metaphors We Die By: How Christian Pacifists Make Better Caregivers" (chapter 4) appeared in the *Toronto Journal of Theology* 19 (2003) 183–97. "Truth in Wittgenstein, Truth in Lindbeck" (chapter 5) appeared in the *Asbury Theological Journal* 57, no. 1 (Fall 2001/Spring 2002) 137–42. "Story and Eucharist: Postliberal Reflections on Anabaptist Nachfolge" (chapter 5) in *Mennonite Quarterly Review* 75 (July 2001) 315–24. "Forester, *Bricoleur*, and Country Bumpkin: Rethinking Knowledge and Habit in Aquinas's Ethics" (chapter 6) © *Scottish Journal of Theology*. Originally published in *Scottish Journal of Theology* 59 (2006) 159–74. Reprinted with permission. I am grateful to these journals and publishers for their kind permission to reprint this material.

PREFACE

"Isn't it a bit early in your career to be publishing your collected works?" I admit I have no witty rejoinder to this friendly question put to me more than once over the past few months. All I can say is that it seemed appropriate to trace out the thematic strand that I think unites these essays and to make it more prominent by having them together in one place.

In bringing these essays together under one cover, I have been able to reflect on the debt of gratitude I owe to the teachers and theological mentors who were close to me as I first drafted them: Samuel Wells, Nancey Murphy, Janet Soskice, Stanley Hauerwas, Glen Stassen, Chris Insole, and the late Paul J. Landa. Even though I am relatively junior within theological scholarship, it is satisfying even now to glance backward, noticing that the road I am on has been made possible by the gracious inspiration and support of these. In their company, I am in their debt.

INTRODUCTION

The theme that unites these essays is speech. It is a theme that is woven in different ways (and in admittedly more and less obvious ways) throughout what follows. I have brought together these writings hoping that they will prove useful for students and practitioners of theology and ethics who are looking for a display of the difference Christian ways of speaking make to the ongoing life of the church in our time.

Christian speech is more normatively prayer, liturgy, and hymnody than it is theology. It is also more straightforwardly witness. When Christian communities speak the gospel, they are performing the truth of their assertions in such a way that their speaking and performing are integrally related. Theology serves this enterprise, thinking the thoughts that undergird the faithful deployment of this task, but can never presume to replace it. As a parasitic discipline, therefore, theology is not just conditioned by its referent—God—but aids a mission: making intelligible the ways that the church must speak if it is to be speaking the gospel. As such, Christian speech is not a deposit—a timeless and frozen vocabulary that trades in erecting fixed structures and impressive systems. There are at least three reasons for this, and they correspond to the ways that Christian speech will display humility, patience, and loyalty.

First, it is true that we love our words. God knows we want them to achieve quite a lot. We have no shortage of words, and they seem to come to us with such ease and in such abundance that it can take some time before we begin to wonder whether we are often just making noise. Certainly we are reluctant to give our words back to God; we would rather keep them and use them for ourselves. But such use will only distort the speaking mission of the church, and so calls for humility. After all, Christians have been invited to speak about things that are beyond words. We speak "God" but are aware that God is a reality that surpasses all terms the definitions of which we are otherwise confident. The problem is not only that what Christians mean by "God" is not shared by everyone else but also that Christians are enjoined to make use of such words even when they refer to something that they cannot contain. And even though we may be driven to silence in the face of God's ineffability—and appropriately so—the Christian community is not permitted to persist that way. I imagine "speak thus" to be God's command to arise from our fitting silence with words that we would not have had if they had not been given to us. Theology must always be prayerful if it is to be true, because we are driven to pray through the chastisement of our speech. Prayer names our refusal to keep our words for ourselves. It is nothing other than the remarkable trust that despite our silence, God would nevertheless have us speak again. The Christian ability to hear "speak thus" as an invitation to speak again will be a function of a humble recognition that we were foolish ever to love our words as our own.

Second, Christian speech can never be thought of as the exclusive property of the church. If the divine Logos, in the incarnation, enters the world as a man, then Christians are permitted to have confidence that the words they must speak about him can likewise enter hostile territory. And its movements from place to place will be marked by the patience necessary to discover the words that are needed in order to say *here* what was said *there*, in order to say *now* what was said *then*. This means that theology will be ongoing: so long as the church has a mission that is still in effect, there will be a theological task. The redemption of the world is partially served by the redemption of the world's ways of speech, which theologians make use of as they seek to animate countless new cultural and linguistic idioms for the sake of the mission that is alive and at work in those idioms.

Christians share words with those outside the church; how could they not? But not all language is equal. Much of what Christians say will be misunderstood by a world that, though it hears familiar words, will not always readily comprehend the unfamiliar message that those words articulate. In his book *The Spirit of Early Christian Thought*, Robert Louis Wilken observes that from the beginning Christian ways of speaking were funded by the richness of Scripture's language. "What the Bible spoke of could not be expressed apart from its unique language and its singular history."[1] For example, Wilken notes that God's nature may be described

---

1. Wilken, *Spirit of Early Christian Thought*, 76.

by Plotinus as "inexhaustible infinity" and "boiling over with life," or by Gregory of Nyssa using the biblical language of "living water." And yet the question is not simply which choice of language better expresses things. Instead,

> What is significant is that "living water" is found in the Bible and would always be found in the Bible. Metaphors and images and symbols drawn from elsewhere, no matter how apt, do not stir the Christian imagination in the same way as those drawn from the Scriptures. . . . Because the words of the Bible endure, they provided scaffolding on which to construct the edifice of Christian thought.[2]

Christians do not claim to know the nature of God apart from language like "living water." Their preference for one form of language over another does not come from standing neutrally before all linguistic options and freely choosing from among them. The church's missionary task depends on its ability to stand on the scaffolding of God-talk that speaks more truth than we can know even while commending that truth to those outside the church by experimenting with different language.[3]

The patient work of God's people who nevertheless keep speaking is itself part of the gospel's witness to the world. And just as the words God invites us to speak are gifts, so also the patient church will not be surprised when its struggle to proclaim the gospel in a new time and place yields insights about its own message that it had not seen before, but that are exposed precisely within and by the new language it is making use of. This is the patience to receive unexpected gifts in the confidence that God's Logos precedes the church's mission, going before and ahead of it in the world. In *Speak Thus*, I have included "On Hauerwas and Yoder" because it investigates the ways that these two theologians similarly, but at points differently, propose to negotiate questions about the kind of public voice the church ought to have. "Democracy Beyond Democracy," a response to Jeffrey Stout's penetrating book, *Democracy and Tradition*, is a test case for the ways such a voice may be made to function within modern, democratic discourse. These engagements and

---

2. Ibid., 77.
3. In his prologue to *On Christian Theology*, Rowan Williams speaks about theology's "communicative" mode in this way.

negotiations are located within the church's ongoing mission, but beyond the work of theology proper.

Even so, if theology too is ongoing in this same sense, then surely it will also come to an end. It will have nothing left to say, nothing else to do, when the mission it serves is finished. When all of creation is enfolded in the divine embrace and ceaselessly finds itself in prayer and praise, theology will cease. Christian speech that is schooled in patience and exercised by receiving unexpected gifts from surprising sources will be better equipped to stop doing theology and start singing. Which means, of course, that theologians *especially* had better start singing now. This book is meant to help us see the madness of ever thinking otherwise.

Third, while the Christian mission—served by theology—advances with a fresh message that is forever good *news*, never expiring or becoming "old news" and therefore always timely, it is always rightly tied to its own past. The mission does not begin from scratch with every new generation and the latest environment. Each setting will present new challenges, but the ability of the church to identify its addressing them as part of its continuous mission will, at least partially, owe to its continuity with where its mission has carried it thus far. When theological discourse has not shied away from its own tradition, it has not always done so for this salutary reason, perhaps often misplacing its confidence in the frozen details of its carefully worked out schemas. But this is only one way and one reason to appeal to the authority of the tradition. We may be much more sanguine about the debt we owe to it since it is only on the basis of having learned to speak one way proficiently that we may, with confidence, improvise—linguistically and otherwise—in a new setting. I am calling this aspect of Christian speech "loyalty" in order to stress the limits to which Christians rightly submit their freedom, out of trust that the church God has created is not forever being abandoned over and over again.

The disunity of the church as it now exists obviously raises an acute difficulty with respect to this claim. But even so, our loyalty to a divided church will surely demonstrate our hope that God has not abandoned it even though we will find ourselves nourishing and nourished by a loyalty to something that does not now fully exist. Improvising on the basis of such a fractured tradition may, therefore, strike us as deplorably reckless. How can we, with confidence, advance the mission of the church in the world, a mission whose advance demands sharp skills honed by practice, when we are seemingly so ill-equipped? How can Christians be ready to face uncertainty when they can only claim a relatively feeble formation? I admit that I do not have a dazzling answer to this except to ask, what else can we do? The church advances with the church it has, not the church it wants. And what is even more frightening is to consider that maybe the church we want is not the church God wants. After all, we will surely want a church that is stronger than God has promised; we will be tempted to turn the advance of the Christian mission into a crusade. "Sheep among wolves" (Matt 10:16) is not only a horrific image; it is also the church's program of dispossession, certainly of violence, but perhaps also—painful as it is—of the unity we seek.

Still, all of this talk can give the impression that God actually *has* abandoned the church to flounder with limited resources, to make the best of less than ideal circumstances. But if the church finds itself in situations it can only describe in this way (as I believe it must in twenty-first-century America if it is going to speak truthfully), then this may not be an indication that God has abandoned it, but precisely that God is present to it, holding forth a unique challenge not to look elsewhere. I have included "Story and Eucharist" in order to show how Swiss Anabaptists in the sixteenth century found the resources they needed to carry on despite a fractured and fracturing church. I am aware that the Anabaptist tradition is often thought of as "reckless" and as anything but loyal. But with the help of Ludwig Wittgenstein's account of the relation between language and practice, together with George Lindbeck's work in *The Nature of Doctrine*, I hope it will be evident that such recklessness is not finally careless. Christian loyalty to our forebears will mean looking for and expecting to find the resources that we thought we could do without, that we thought we abandoned for good reasons in our attempts to be "relevant." This book endeavors to affirm ways that Christians are rediscovering these resources in the realization that nothing, in fact, could be more relevant to a world that is perishing without the humble, patient, and loyal witness of God's people.

## BECOMING TRUTHFUL

God speaks first. Only then do Christians share in the speech of God, the speech that creates and continues to uphold creation. And the way Christians do this is by sharing in the church. In the book of Acts, the sign of God's creation of the church is the tongues of fire that accompanied the gift of the Holy Spirit that fell on the gathered disciples-turned-apostles. In an important sense, the tongues of fire *are themselves* the gift of the Holy Spirit insofar as the apostles were given the spirit of Christ, the word of God. When the church speaks, therefore, not only does it speak by the power of the Holy Spirit, but its very speech is the *action* of the Spirit. This is to say that the speech that creates the church is continuous with the language that the church is invited to inhabit in its proclamation to the world.

We can make some sense of this dual claim christologically. Christians confess that Christ is the Word of God, the agent of creation, the one by whom and for whom everything that exists, exists. In the incarnation, the word became flesh, and yet the word has been raised from the dead; the ascension of the Word into heaven did not permanently remove the word from the earth. Just as Christ was incarnate by the Holy Spirit, he was once again made present in the world by the Holy Spirit at Pentecost. *That* word is simultaneously the church itself and the church's proclamation. Put differently, the risen Christ has a body, and that body is the church.[4] But the church can never exist apart from its proclamation since the latter is also the word of God by which the church is constituted. This means that the church is only church insofar as its very existence attests to the life, death, and resurrection of Christ. For this reason, Robert Jenson is right to follow the Vatican II documents in describing the church as a kind of sacrament. Since a sacrament both points to and is the thing it signifies, we may say that "the church points to Christ and so—and only so—is Christ."[5] When the church ceases to point to Christ, it becomes just another club, embarrassingly evacuated of its identity and purpose.

A community's ability to abide in the speech of God will depend on its ability to inhabit the truth of its words. By drawing on some aspects of Radical Orthodoxy and insights from narrative theology, "Narrative Proclamation and Gospel Truthfulness" asks about the kind of knowledge Christian witness names and the status of its truth. I show that our ability to give an accurate rendering of these things is hampered both by modern epistemology and by the ways that such accounts are ineluctably bound up with sovereign power and the legitimacy of state violence.

---

4. Jenson, "Church and the Sacraments," 209.
5. Ibid., 212.

In contrast, when Christians confess (in both senses of the word), we are being the most truthful, as Augustine maintained. We are caught up in an activity whose truth is larger than our abilities to assent with full knowledge to the objects of our confession. The confession of God's glory in adoration, and of human sinfulness in penitent sadness, both confront the Christian with what is real and true. Words of confession spoken back to God constitute the highest instance of truth telling. This does not mean that nothing else Christians say can be true, but that the truth of anything else that may be spoken will derive its intelligibility from lives otherwise rooted in the life of a community that openly subjects itself to the linguistic discipline that worship names. So while Christian speech—the offering of God's words back to God—may never constitute all our speech this side of heaven, it nevertheless is paradigmatic for understanding how we ought to relate to words generally.

Human speech is not "natural" since we do not naturally turn to God in worship, preferring idols instead. We do not naturally want what is not natural to us. But saying this can also distort the complex relationship between nature and grace. "Forester, *Bricoleur*, and Country Bumpkin" investigates this complexity in the moral thought of Thomas Aquinas, and "This is My Brother's World" examines nature and grace in relation to creation. While not always explicitly making reference to Karl Barth, these chapters both present Barthian readings. Interrogating the complexity of nature and grace hopefully clarifies some things, but I will not pretend that this necessarily makes the task of Christians any easier. Even though we may not naturally want what is not natural to us, part of the Christian hope must be that God's grace is not ultimately at odds with our nature. We have a complicated task even though God's gifts for abiding in the speech of God have already been given; they are available to be used. If the church's first mode of speech is its praise and adoration of God, it learns how to speak through worship and liturgy. Its ritual performances are often partially linguistic. The church at prayer and the church at proclamation are two different things even as they enrich each other, just as it is impossible to imagine a church that only prays and does not proclaim, or vice versa. The reading and hearing of Scripture is more than an exercise in literacy since we must be taught how to read *Scripture*, how this reading differs from reading the newspaper or a novel, how we ought to relate to what is read, why it has authority over us, and how to keep reading the parts we particularly do not want.

Singing, of course, is a particularly involved form of reading, which reminds us that Christian ritual performances are also partially bodily. Christians continue to read and sing *all* the psalms and not just the ones that bring us comfort or conform to our tendency to think of ourselves as generally righteous. For example, by persisting in singing "Happy shall he be who takes your little ones and dashes them against the rock!" (Ps 137:9), we learn that we cannot escape singing these words *as our own*. We cannot pass them off as somebody else's words—words of someone more depraved, less righteous, more in distress, less comfortable. And we come to learn this partially through the act of singing them since our whole bodies are enlisted in making this declaration. Our singing is itself also disciplined by the variety of things we are made to sing, especially those things we would not have chosen to sing on our own.

Even though our ritual performances are both linguistic and bodily, these two are not finally separable since it is our bodies that speak when "we" speak. We are therefore habituated into a style of speaking that is itself a style of being in the world. In other words, Christians have not so much been told what to say; we have been taught how to speak: shown style and cadence, trained in the ways to intone and inflect.

### POSITIVE SPEECH AS RESISTANCE

An additional element animates the essays compiled here. I hope that what I have to say in *Speak Thus* will be thought of as *positive*, by which I mean that they acknowledge and explore the positive existence of the church in the world. Questions about Christian identity and integrity will not be answered by a defensive church that takes antagonism with the world as a first principle, its agenda forever being shaped in response to crises in the world. This is not to say that Christians ought to be insular or to disregard worldly crises; but it is to say that so long as Christian existence is determined by such crises, the world is without its best hope. For example, Austrian filmmaker Hans Weingartner portrays a compelling drama of youthful enthusiasm for social justice in his 2004 production, *Fetten Jahre sind vorbei*.[6] He explores the revolutionary spirit behind a small group of twenty-somethings dedicated to bringing down capitalism, one rich person at a time. In one of the film's more wistful moments, Jan, the most wide eyed of the bunch, is offered a mind-numbing narcotic

---

6. Weingarten, *Die Fetten Jahre sind vorbei*.

but declines it, urging that drug use dampens the revolutionary drive. He cannot compromise the work that needs to be done for the cause, and so his mind and body must be kept alert. Jan is not *against* drugs; he was *for* the revolution.

Christian reflection would benefit from just so positive an account of the *raison d'être* of Christian mission: a way of life so riveting on account of its endlessly fascinating object and absorbing purposes that all subsequent behaviors, attitudes, and modes of being are taken into its account. Nancy Reagan cheated a generation of American schoolchildren when she exhorted them, "Just say no to drugs." The grandness of the "no," with all of its clear-sighted, oppositional resonances, however, was not how she cheated them; it was the enervating "just." That "just" signified that there is no revolution, no way of life worth living that makes drug use unthinkable. Swords are not beaten into ploughshares by a people who "just" reject war, but by a people who would rather farm. What American children needed was not Mrs. Reagan's moralistic rule but another option—a positive activity so compelling that many others become distractions. Children were absorbed with drugs not out of ignorance or perversity but out of boredom; Mrs. Reagan's "just" only reinforced that boredom. Christian ethics has too often assumed that the Christian life is just as boring as the after-school hours in America. Boredom, of course, is just another way of indicating a lack of imagination.

In the last half century, philosophical reflection on language, ethical retrieval of virtue, and a certain kind of sociological and ethnographic investigation have led to an emphasis on practice. Jan's revolution, like athletics for American children, is a practice in this sense. Such practices invite systematic reflection for discovering the resources that they offer for resisting competing practices too easily taken for granted and insufficiently resisted by more direct methods. In this book, I hope that it will be evident how much we still have to learn from the practices we have been given and, in particular, how they enhance the church's witness through their own integrity.

But I also suspect a danger in too readily reaching after practices, Christian or otherwise. This can surely invite descriptions of varying depth, which can be a problem since we do not know, in any obvious way, how to speak about what we are doing. When in "Metaphors we Die By," for example, I discuss the practice of caring for the ill and dying, it is the very description of that practice—the metaphors employed in describing—that comes into question in the hopes of suggesting that our descriptions are also partially constitutive of what it is we are doing. So whereas Christian care for the ill may sometimes look just like everyone else's care, the ability to narrate it differently is both a function of and a contribution to its very real difference. As I suggest in that chapter, nonviolence will be bound up with Christian care of the sick, and not only linguistically.

Nevertheless I have not gone out of my way to describe these essays as "ethics." There are two reasons for this. First, as an academic discipline, ethics still too often can take itself to be a primary set of concerns. Questions about how to live (questions too often divorced from a consideration of the traditions to which such commitments belong, from the character of the communities that share in and therefore extend those traditions, and the virtues engendered by active membership in them) somehow continue to pass as "ethical." Second, though I will reluctantly accept the nomenclature of ethics even while protesting its impoverished nature as it is still usually conceived, my preference for advancing and engaging the language of the Christian faith as a first-order discourse cannot accurately be described as anything but theology proper. I am quite happy with this categorization, especially as it aids in emphasizing a point made from the opposite direction, namely, that Christian theology never exists for its own sake. It may never busy itself with intellectual games and academic exercises with an end in view that only leaves more work for other academics. After all, as I have already intimated, theology itself is tied to the church's proclamation and, as such, inherently resists being turned in upon itself. The sermons at the end of this book are intended to display this. I like to preach and am always grateful for the chance to do it. As a lay theologian, I know that preaching is not my primary work if for no other reason than that I must be invited to preach by those for whom it is their primary work. But by including sermons in this book, I hope to indicate that the line between theology and the proclamation it is meant to enable should not be one that is easily drawn.

It may sound absurd, but theology is for the world. Yet it is only ever for the world inasmuch as the church continues to try to speak about God truthfully. I trust that such comments make it clear that an emphasis on the church's own speech must never be described as parochial. The quality of the church's discourse must instead always depend on the manner in which it is spoken *for the sake of the world*, but not by way of taking the world's speech as a starting point since the world does not have the word of God, absent the witness of Christ in the church. The separation of proclamation from theology, therefore, impoverishes both proclamation and theology. Christian theology, like Christian ethics, is one way that the church is reminded that it does not exist only for itself. But only to the extent that the church continually refines its life together—in order to inhabit its linguistic habits to serve its life together as a primary way of speaking—will it have anything worth saying to the world.

# NEGOTIATING

CHAPTER 1

*Narrative Proclamation and Gospel Truthfulness*

I

Let us begin with an observation that is at home within Radical Orthodoxy: Written texts can be misleading insofar as what they report can be imagined as free-floating facts, events, or ideas; that is, unbounded by the realities of cultural existence, of conditions surrounding both the production and reading of texts. This observation makes plain the ways we may be tempted to draw a straight line from the meaning of a text to the truth of that meaning, assuming that both can be exhaustively captured and assessed on the basis of the written word alone.

Radical Orthodoxy pursues these kinds of hermeneutical questions in order to show two things. First, it shows that texts themselves are not the sole bearers of their own meaning. Therefore, questions of a text's truth cannot be answered on the basis of texts alone.[1] Second, it helps us imagine domains of truth and meaning that are embodied in time. These are, as Catherine Pickstock argues, ultimately enacted in worship and praise.[2] The pasts intended to be reported in written texts are taken up into the present-tense actions of people for whom the truth of statements is not separable from their own participation in the truth. Though it sounds strange to put it this way, the worship of God is therefore "more true" than anything that can be said about it. This is because as long as meaning and truth are allowed to float free of people's cultural and historical existences, such people will only awkwardly and inauthentically find themselves attesting to such meanings and truths through maintain-

---

1. This, of course, is not a unique contribution of Radical Orthodoxy, but is adopted from some strains of continental postmodern philosophy.

2. Pickstock, *After Writing*.

ing a distance from them. Such distance is only traversed in practice. Speech is better than writing, then, since there is a temporal immediacy between words and actions and, therefore, speakers (unlike writers) cannot escape the meanings and consequences of their own words as they speak them. The truth of statements is thus bound up with the truthfulness of speakers.

II

These prefatory comments rightly lead us into our main topic—a discussion of witnesses. Witnesses who swear to tell the truth in a law court indicate a connection between witness and truthfulness. But what can we say about this connection? We may agree with Hannah Arendt that some things can only be known through the testimonies of witnesses. The fragile nature of facts that could be otherwise makes testimony the necessary mode of their transmission: "Factual truths are never compellingly true. . . . Facts need testimony to be remembered and trustworthy witnesses to be established in order to find a secure dwelling place in the domain of human affairs."[3] This is especially the case with unusual events, those things that violate our assumptions about the way the world normally works, about cause and effect, about ranges of possibility. Therefore if we are to know such things, there will need to be people who tell the truth in their testimony, and there will also need to be people who trust that they are speaking truthfully.

The trouble is that we would rather not have to trust witnesses. We would prefer to be able to subject the testimonies we hear to a more incontrovertible mode of knowledge, one that is attained and sustained with greater certainty. We would rather be able to rely on the confidence afforded by science, with its comprehensive explanations and its ability to give accounts of otherwise mysterious facts on the basis of its grand theories. After all, why should we trust witnesses? In the real world, testimonies notoriously contradict one another; witnesses have selective memories and end up reporting some facts and not others. Our legal system makes use of juries and judges because it cannot be the case that every testimony will be true. Answering the question about the connection between witness and truthfulness, therefore, begins to take the form

---

3. Arendt, *Crises of the Republic*, 6.

of appeals for certainty: appeals to certify the truth of what is spoken, to guarantee that witnesses will not lie, and to catch them when they do.

But our appeal to the idiom of courtrooms and trials actually intensifies our question. Judges and juries make appeal to a body of law in order to determine the truth of testimony. Not only does law exist as a prior set of codes that help make such determinations, but those who pass judgment on the truth of testimony exist in their roles by virtue of how the law is embodied institutionally. From the physical structures of courthouses and the elevated chairs of judges to the national guilds of legal professionals with their exams and licenses to practice—all of these institutions are constituted by the fact that laws exist, and their existence requires institutional support.

Consider, for example, how oath taking is one such institution that supervenes rather directly on the giving and hearing of testimony. We even began this essay by observing that *swearing* to tell the truth indicates the connection between truthfulness and witness. But what if the oath is only ancillary to the truthfulness of witnesses and not internal to it at all? In this respect, we have only to notice that an oath does not actually guarantee true testimony. All it does is ensure that the words about to be spoken will submit themselves to legal discipline should they be found to be false within the legal sphere into which testimony is given. Lies become perjury when spoken under oath, and perjury is taken to be more serious than lying because it entails more severe legal consequences. In other words, oaths subordinate testimony to sovereign authority.

On the surface, an oath seems to be an exercise that is prior to and separate from testimony. Oaths function as a prior justification and guarantee of what is about to be spoken. But we immediately need to correct this impression since any explanation of the subsequent discourse is part of that discourse, not prior to it. The truthfulness in which the oath is spoken cannot be greater than the truth of the testimony it is meant to control. This means that nothing can be said in addition to a true testimony in order to guarantee that it will be true. Put differently, it is more important to tell the truth than to *promise* to tell the truth (since even a promise to tell the truth must be told truthfully if it is to have any meaning). When oaths are sworn in courts, the introduction of an allegedly higher standard (symbolized by the oath) that denotes the subsequent possibility of perjury really introduces a *lower* standard for speech that is *not* spoken under oath. Another way to make the same point is to say that the practice of oath-taking depends on justifying oaths quite apart from justifying truthfulness. A person will generally be persuaded to swear an oath for reasons that are different from the reasons he may have for speaking the truth. Jesus's teaching on oaths in the Sermon on the Mount (Matt 5:33–37) even seems to indicate that oaths are often taken in order to avoid doing what is promised. Moreover, people who think more is at stake for speaking truthfully when under oath are less likely to have their characters formed according to the commitment to speak the truth all the time.

Heirs of the radical Reformation, such as Anabaptists and Quakers, sometimes faced severe opposition for their resistance to oath-taking. Anabaptists in particular found that by resisting taking oaths, they were resisting the authorities, who understood oaths to be a foundation of civil society. This was a perspective shared by Reformers such as Luther, Melanchthon, and Heinrich Bullinger.[4] A seventeenth-century Puritan offers a clear example of the ways that oaths serve ruling authorities:

> Oaths are necessary for the execution of the magistrate's office and the preservation of human society. For without such oaths the commonwealth hath no surety upon public officers and ministers: nor kings upon their subjects; nor lords upon their tenants; neither can men's titles be cleared in causes civil, nor justice done in causes criminal; nor dangerous plots and conspiracies be discovered against the state.[5]

It is striking that the emphasis here is not on *truthfulness* as the basis of civil society, but on *the oath*. It is the guarantee that is most important since the guarantee is an acknowledgement of who has authority to punish, who has a right to the truth, in which setting, on what matters, and so on. An oath pays homage to the one who is responsible for the security brought by the binding nature of an oath and the punishment that attends to perjury. But as the Anabaptists and others discovered, oaths then become more important than the truth itself. It is easy to commit perjury, but it is very difficult to refuse to swear an oath, especially when one might face being put to death as a heretic.[6] Against this, those

---

4. Bullinger called the oath "the bond, which holds together the whole body of the common good of just government." (quoted in Kreider, "Christ, Culture, and Truth Telling," 217).

5. Daniel Featly, *The Dippers Dipt*, quoted in ibid.

6. Ibid., 218.

who refused oaths took their understanding of truthful speech from the Sermon on the Mount: "Let what you say be simply 'Yes' or 'No'; anything more than this comes from evil" (Matt 5:37). Jesus's disciples should not look for ways of making their speech true or of certifying it apart from speaking truly since an oath is redundant in the face of true testimony. Oaths condition truthful speech in the same way that theories of truth condition truth—both rely on what they purport to control. Oaths safeguard the truthfulness of the truth in advance of testimony, betraying a reliance on the power of magistrates—and ultimately on the sword—at the expense of the power of a truthfully spoken "yes" and "no."[7]

In a sense, therefore, oaths are posturing and bluffing. They accomplish nothing because they are just an exercise of power that obtains only insofar as testimony is connected to power.

But what about testimony that is given irrespective of power relations and the violence that undergirds them? For Christians, this is not an abstract or merely academic question since it touches directly on our mission in the world: bearing witness to the good news of Christ. Christians have been commissioned to proclaim to the world the resurrection of the Son of God, to make him known by word and deed, to attest before and for the world that salvation is in Christ, that the world belongs to him, and that his works are good. Christians undertake this without submitting their testimonies to the requirements of sovereignty—indeed, do so in the face of such sovereignty, inasmuch as the gospel is a direct assault on the pride of the nations.

III

How else might we speak about truthfulness and testimony? In many aspects of modern philosophy and conventional wisdom is a preoccupation with questions about how something can be known, and how it can be known to be true. The former is explicitly within the domain described

---

7. Some common expressions such as "and that's the gospel truth" function in the same way. Furthermore, oaths are based on lying. As the Quaker William Penn observed, where there is no lying, there is no need to govern testimony by oaths: "[I]f Christians ought never to lie, it is most certain that they need never to swear; for swearing is built upon lying; take away lying, and there remains no more ground for swearing; truth-speaking comes in the room thereof." *A Treatise of Oaths: Containing Several Weighty Reasons Why People called Quakers Refuse to Swear* (1675), in *Selected Works*, vol. 2 (1825), 44, cited in ibid., 218–19.

by epistemology and the latter takes knowledge of the truth to be a subset of epistemological questions, or at least a function of our ability to answer those questions. This construction implies, for one, that we would seem to be entitled to believe that something is true only insofar as we are able to prove its truth; we can only claim to know something if we can demonstrate that it is "knowable." This immediately foregrounds some related political questions. Possible justifications for true beliefs must then include all rational people since justifications must appeal to some shared criterion beyond the belief in question. Viewed from this perspective, people who doubt an (allegedly) justified belief are thought to be irrational, as they have not merely rejected the belief, but also the entire structure of shared reason that grounded the belief in the first place. The irrationality of others is political because it is how we make clear that *they* are not one of *us*.

As a result, so long as those who deliver a testimony accept these requirements of justification for the truth of what they say, they will find themselves making two kinds of statements. The first kind of statement is, in some sense, the more basic—it is the testimony itself, the eye-witness report, "This is what I saw. . . ." But taken alone, this will not be enough, since a second kind of statement will also be needed. That second kind is the statement that justifies the testimony, the rationale for why it is true, the account of why it should be believed, the explanation for how it counts as knowledge. This two-tier construction is so prevalent that those who dare to speak the first kind of statement without the second, that is, those who speak testimony without justifying it according to reason are themselves accounted as irrational or fideistic. Not only do they believe what they say because of a faith that responds to the peace and beauty of the truth, but they also hope that others will believe it on the same basis. In the face of modern epistemology, this can only be seen as an affront to reason itself. It comes as no surprise, therefore, that faith and reason have been set up in opposition to each other.

But some serious questions have been raised against the ascendancy of this two-tiered epistemology in recent years. Here we may probe some of the inadequacies inherent in constructing knowledge according to a model that privileges justification. In particular, because Christians are witnesses rather than judges, issues of justification are not immediately suited to the Christian mission of making Christ known to the world. In fact, making Christ *known* has nothing to do with explaining the testimony about him. Our ability to clarify how this is the case has been greatly enriched by the work of Radical Orthodox theologians and their associates. For example, as John Milbank observes when discussing Paul Ricoeur, "'Narrating' . . . turns out to be a more basic category than either explanation or understanding."[8] Testimony tells a narrative that is *temporally structured* and, while it usually cannot point to its necessity on the basis of universal laws and first causes, it *can* point to antecedent causes and what has (contingently) followed from them—what comes immediately before and after.[9] As with characters or readers within a story that is not yet finished, we do not judge at a remove from the story itself but only on the basis of what has been given through the story. If we could draw conclusions from what went before (that is, without narrating subsequent developments in plot), we would not wonder, what happens next? Christian witness thus is in the strange position of declaring the truth about Christ without containing him, of narrating a true story without being able to lay claim to its definitive interpretation or the exact nature of its conclusion.

Dispossessed of the force of explanation, however, Christians are nevertheless not off the hook with respect to their mission to the nations since the proclamation of the gospel is characterized by peaceful invitation rather than by the assertion of power in the guise of rationality. Therefore, Christians may make selective use of postmodern thought in order to overcome certain totalizing and pretentious elements of modern thought. As David Bentley Hart comments, Christian thought "has no stake in the myth of disinterested rationality," rightly suspecting that the epistemological project of modernity is a ruse for power.[10] Against this, Hart goes on to argue that "postmodern theory confirms theology in its original condition: that of a story, thoroughly dependent upon a sequence of historical events to which the only access is the report and practice of believers, a story whose truthfulness may be urged—even enacted—but never proved simply by the process of scrupulous dialectic."[11] The story of Christ come and risen cannot be demonstrated according to the force

---

8. Milbank, *Theology and Social Theory*, 267.

9. See also Hauerwas, *Truthfulness and Tragedy*, 28–29.

10. Hart, *Beauty of the Infinite*, 4. There seems to be no consensus on whether Hart should be counted among the ranks of Radical Orthodoxy. However, enough points of contact with Radical Orthodoxy justify using Hart as I do here.

11. Ibid.

of reason; the church is equipped with "no means whereby to corroborate its wildly implausible claim, except the demonstrative practice of Christ's peace."[12] Therefore, when the peaceful offer of the Christian proclamation is rejected by others, we cannot attribute such rejection to their irrationality, but to their sin, that is, to their exercise of freedom before God to reject God. This kind of attribution is crucial to the peaceable offer that Christian proclamation makes since the temptation to overcome and overwhelm human freedom in the name of rationality is a form of violence.

It is important to see how what we have said about oath taking and power relates to the modern preoccupation with epistemological certainty. Both are ways of ensuring true speech, though neither operates at the level of the testimony itself. Both, in fact, hover above testimony, only making contact with it at points that are conditioned by either the threat or the actual exercise of violence and coercion. Oaths become incoherent when divorced from a system of power that can enforce them. This is why courtroom oaths only have the appearance of swearing to God, when in fact they are a way of affirming the authority of the state and its right to use force in the name of securing the truth.

But surely we are left wondering what to do when we are presented with conflicting testimonies. On the one hand, it seems quite absurd to ask, "Well, did they swear to tell the truth? If so, then they are telling the truth." This is because if someone is determined to lie at the level of testimony, they are likely also to lie at the level of the oath. Put differently, this logic only works if the witness's loyalty to the truth of her testimony is no stronger than her loyalty to the government. On the other hand, it is less absurd to ask, "How can we be sure that what we have heard is true? How can these witnesses know what they claim to know?" This is clearly less absurd since we are bound to rely on these kinds of judgments despite our waning confidence in oaths. Nevertheless, such questions are still one step removed from testimony itself and so find themselves either operating on an epistemological level of proofs and evidence or, in the philosophical realm, relying on theories of knowledge and truth.

---

12. Ibid., 3.

IV

In order to make more concrete some of these comments about knowledge, witness, and truth, it is interesting to consider the 1950 Japanese film by Akira Kurosawa, *Rashômon*. The film tells the stories of several witnesses to a rape and a murder. But rape and murder are not what makes the film disturbing and, as many of its first viewers thought, even morally objectionable. Instead, it is the way that the conflicting testimonies of the witnesses are portrayed. Until *Rashômon*, audiences were accustomed to taking for granted that what they saw portrayed was the reality internal to the film itself. Seeing was believing, even though it was occasionally violated by plot elements such as the discovery that it was all a dream. But Kurosawa deliberately presented viewers with several conflicting testimonies: by an eyewitness, by the rape victim, by the murder victim (from beyond the grave through a medium), and others. All provided details in which they themselves were implicated in the violence, or in other ways presented facts that were irreconcilable with the other testimonies. At the start of each testimony, the violent scene is shown according to that report. But rather than the camera showing what really happened, the camera merely echoed the words of the conflicting witnesses.

What Kurosawa refused to do was to intervene at the level of adjudication. The camera did not rise above the fray of conflicting witnesses and discordant testimony. Instead, as members of the film's audience, we are actually involved in the film itself in the character of the camera. No omniscient narrator secures the certainty of our vision. Some thought Kurosawa was making the (now monotonous) point that there is no objective truth, but this misconstrues what is conveyed by displaying the conflicting testimonies of witnesses without deciding for us which one is true. As disturbing as *Rashômon* has been for audiences who have wanted to know what really happened, it is striking that the film is only less like films up to that point, and almost mundanely much more like our lives. We are familiar with the fact that we must trust the testimonies of some people if we are to have any knowledge apart from what we have experienced ourselves. Not only this, but we find that we actually need to trust most people to tell the truth most of the time in order to live free from the constant anxiety of continual doubt. Three of the film's characters debate this point:

COMMONER: And I suppose that is supposed to be true.

WOODCUTTER (*getting to his feet*): I don't tell lies. I saw it with my own eyes.

COMMONER: That I doubt.

WOODCUTTER: I don't tell lies.

COMMONER: Well, so far as that goes, no one tells lies after he has said that he is going to tell one.

PRIEST: But it's horrible—if men do not tell the truth, do not trust one another, then the earth becomes a kind of hell.

COMMONER: You are right. The world we live in is a hell.[13]

The priest represents the attempt to draw a conclusion about human behavior (people tell the truth and trust one another) because he fears the kind of world that would be indicated if it were not true (it would be hell). In this sense, the priest seems irretrievably naïve, simply unwilling to admit that the world might actually be what he fears most. By contrast, the commoner seems heroic, courageously facing up to the reality of the world as it really is, unafraid to declare it and determined to continue living life in the face of a hard truth.

But here we see the deeper level of the film. Kurosawa is not actually interested in the question of whether truth is relative or objective. He is interested in what it means to live with human faculties and limitations. We cannot know the details about the murder and the rape, because we were not there. Even those who were there are prejudiced toward their own testimonies because they each have interests bound up with what they say. In other words, we are like the witnesses; like them, we do not see clearly, and our blindness is invested with what it means to be human. Audiences wanted the clear-sighted knowledge they had been used to seeing at the movies, without being reminded of the uncertainty that marks our creaturely existence. Kurosawa would not allow the audience to "escape" human limitation through appeals to greater levels of knowledge.

Kurosawa knew that we would rather be judges than witnesses. In *Rashômon*, the flashback scenes that depict the testimonies are captured by a shaky, hand-held camera, punctuated with glances at the blinding sun. By virtue of this unusual cinematography, audiences are involved

---

13. Kurosawa and Richie, *Rashomon*, 86–87.

in the limited vision of the witnesses, immersed in the tussle that affects vision as much as understanding and judgment. But in the courtroom scenes, the camera is fixed and stable. The questions of the prosecution come from offscreen, and the witnesses answer them by speaking directly into the camera, straight to the audience. In these scenes, we are not the witnesses but the prosecution and judges, interrogating the discordant versions of the story in order to get to the truth. Kurosawa is aware that cinematic convention generally panders to our narcissistic fantasies as judges, but he refuses to sanction the certainty usually afforded to audiences by this juridical mode of storytelling.

*Rashômon* challenged the truth of observation that audiences had hitherto relied on as an unshakable epistemological principle. Instead of the certainty of knowledge being taken for granted, the question of knowledge was recast as a *moral* question. The priest in the story gives voice to this shift. He is not so much concerned with what the fact of conflicting testimonies means for the truth they are meant to declare, nor does he try to harmonize their disparate accounts by overwhelming the fragile (though always possibly false) details they provide. He is primarily interested in what conflicting testimonies tell us about the witnesses themselves.

> PRIEST: But the woman turned up in prison too, you know. It seems she went to seek refuge at some temple and the police found her there. . . .
>
> WOODCUTTER: It's a lie. They're all lies. Tajomaru's confession, the woman's story—they're lies.
>
> COMMONER: Well, men are only men. That's why they lie. They can't tell the truth, not even to themselves.
>
> PRIEST: That may be true. But it's because men are so weak. That's why they lie. That's why they must deceive themselves.
>
> COMMONER: Not another sermon! I don't mind a lie. Not if it's interesting. What kind of story did she tell?
>
> PRIEST: Hers was a completely different story from the bandit's. Everything was different. Tajomaru talked about her temper. I saw nothing like that at all. I found her very pitiful. I felt great compassion for her.[14]

14. Ibid., 62–63.

Both the priest and the commoner agree that lying is bound up with our humanity, but only the commoner is satisfied by his own cynicism over against the priest's compassion for human weakness. Neither of these men is going to solve the problem of epistemology, partly because their conversation has sketched out the way that the problem involves the very aspects of their two characters that they display in that conversation. We might say that cynicism and compassion are the two basic character orientations to the truth of testimony. Both define a relationship to truth, but not by directly interfacing with facts; instead, both relate to the human other from the standpoint of the person of the witness, the one who delivers testimony.

V

How shall we appropriate these insights to a discussion of the Christian testimony? Christian witnesses are indispensable because what they tell cannot be known apart from testimony. That God raised Jesus from the dead cannot be deduced through logic or arrived at on the basis of a theory about how the world works. The details of testimony are contingent, which is to say, they might have been otherwise. Witnesses claim that the details were this way as opposed to that, though they cannot certify their claims by appealing to anything more stable and convincing than their testimonies. One of the positive and constructive aspects of postmodern developments is precisely the declining legitimacy of totalizing metanarratives, leaving Christians with only a narrative proclamation, which is all that Christians have ever had anyway.[15] Our postmodern situation highlights the ways that Christian testimony narrates details without claiming to know what they all mean. Testimony claims that Jesus is risen, without exhaustively laying claim to the nature of resurrection. This is what we see in the New Testament: a refusal to *explain* what a resurrection is but nevertheless affirming it by narrating the change it enacts and inaugurates. In the same way, the narrative proclamation of Christ does not rest on comprehensive explanations but remains open to the possibility that the resurrection may yet continue to disclose itself in new ways in the world. A risen Christ will continue to act in unexpected ways, which points to

---

15. Of course Christians have often purported to have more than this, and, in fact, some forms of modern philosophy were based precisely on a certain comfort with construing some Christian beliefs according to necessary reason.

how the resurrection is not only a historical occurrence but a confession that reality is full of surprise. But this is only another way of saying that what is real is created full of variety and promise, that what is created is a gift always insufficiently laid hold of even by our most ingenious efforts.

Then again, Christian testimony is more than a set of eternal truths disclosed by the reality of Christ. It resists being construed in general terms as, for example, pointing to more fundamental notions such as love, suffering, and compassion. Instead, Christian testimony is irreducibly particular; there is nothing more fundamental than the facts it tells.

We should admit that this seems like a paradox. On the one hand, Christian witness refuses to lay claim to general, foundational notions for its justification; on the other hand, it testifies to the inexhaustibility of the substance of its own testimony. Christ is not a symbol of something else, and yet to speak of Christ is to speak of a fullness that cannot be exhausted by what we say about him. Put differently, Christ is the shape of all reality and yet is only disclosed through the particular instances and claims that are given to Christians to proclaim.

Though this sounds paradoxical, it is only a paradox according to the way that modern philosophy and conventional wisdom would have us think about the truth of testimonies, that is, the knowledge of witnesses. Testimonies were meant to explain things, or otherwise were meant to be validated on some grounds other than their own truth. But such validation could only be achieved at the expense of unique testimony, that is, at the expense of testimonies that would speak anything genuinely new. When something is known because it accords with our prior understanding about how the world works, such workings can never be the subject of critique. And when something is known because it is submitted to the control of sovereign power, the absoluteness of that power's authority can only be questioned by risking the offer of testimony unsupported by the guarantees institutionally enshrined by that power. Both the inflated claims of epistemology and power-imbued legal protocols are set against Christian testimony insofar as Christians attest to a reality that is unbounded and free. The proclamation of Christ's resurrection is bound up with the confession that he is sovereign over the nations and that they are subject to his judgment. But precisely because worldly sovereignty is exposed as pretentious are Christians therefore enabled to appear as witnesses rather than as judges.

Testimony of the risen Christ is an invitation to others to look again at the world with wide-eyed expectation. If Christ is risen, then the proclamation that he is risen will always speak of Christ in the present tense: Christian testimony does not just narrate historical facts of the past but discloses the reality of the present. Moreover, the church's ability to proclaim at all is part of that present reality. The church does not simply tell a story *about* Christ, but the telling is part of the content of its proclamation insofar as the risen Christ is free to surprise the church in its own speech. Proclaiming the resurrection is therefore inseparable from giving an account of how it is that Christ speaks now in this very proclamation, since anything less than the coincidence of Christ's speech and our proclamation of the resurrection would demonstrate that the resurrection is not true.[16] Christian proclamation must therefore respect the freedom of the risen Christ since the substance of the testimony itself attests to the unpredictable actions that Christ will continue to perform insofar as he is alive. A living person will act freely in ways that are not knowable simply by knowing the person. In this, Christian witness holds that Christ is knowable not only as a historical occurrence but as an abiding reality. So a consequence of the claim that Christ is risen and is therefore alive is that he can surprise us; that he can be known, but that because he is living and will act freely, he cannot be anticipated or predicted.[17] We never know what he will do next, except insofar as he binds himself to his promises.[18] The resurrected Christ must be attested by a people who expect him to exercise the freedom that comes with being alive. Sometimes dissatisfied with the lack of control this involves, Christian witness will be tempted to condition its own testimony in one way or another in order to make it more convincing or, at its strongest, irrefutable.

But it remains that what Christians believe and proclaim to the world cannot be known apart from witnesses. If it could, then it would

---

16. Nevertheless it is not possible to demonstrate the truth of the resurrection by any means, though its plausibility can be attested by a people whose life together is characterized by a free, living Christ. The impossibility of demonstration is exactly what we would expect, given the logic of resurrection.

17. See Jenson, *Systematic Theology*, 1:198.

18. The *Schleitheim Confession* argues against oath taking on grounds that while God is able to keep his promises under his own power, we are not. In this way, we might go on to say that human faith knows the future of God insofar as God has made promises about some things. This is another reminder that knowledge is relational, and that the freedom of God to surprise is only ever limited by God's will to hold himself to his word.

not be true.¹⁹ This is because God has created and redeemed the world through sheer contingency: he did not have to create; he did not have to redeem. The actions of God in the world cannot be explained through extrapolation or logical argument. Moreover, Jesus did not rise from the dead for "reasons" that could be offered as proof apart from the fragility of those who attest that Jesus is risen. That Christ's witnesses risk being ignored, disbelieved, or silenced through martyrdom is inherent in the gift God has given the world by refusing to overpower human freedom. The fact that some will believe and others will not is not a function of Christian failure to anchor its proclamation in something more solid and convincing than the contingency of the church's own existence. Instead, the existence of the church already attests to the reality of a nonnecessary creation. Just as God did not need to create the world, Jesus did not need to call disciples, and God did not need to create the church. And since the church's continued existence depends on proclaiming the gospel for the sake of the new belief of each generation, the connection between proclamation and the success of the church's witness is one of promise and gift. For those who have inherited the radical-Reformation tradition in one way or another, it may not be difficult to grasp how the Christian ability to resist sovereign power (particularly when it is abusive in its pretentious claims) will depend on the ability of Christians to persist in offering peaceful, unbounded testimony to the world.

---

19. However this statement, as with the sentence marked by footnote 16 above, must not be construed as a proof of Christian truth. See Hauerwas, *With the Grain of the Universe*, 207.

CHAPTER 2

## *On Hauerwas and Yoder*

Stanley Hauerwas has claimed that "Everything John Howard Yoder believes, I think is true."[1] Indeed, this is also a common assumption regarding the two theologians since Hauerwas is better known and also makes plain his indebtedness to Yoder in nearly every essay and book. However, Craig Carter recently wrote that "The biggest problem in Yoder interpretation arises with regard to Stanley Hauerwas."[2] This is because many readers come to Yoder by way of Hauerwas and, as a consequence, impose an interpretive grid whereby the differences between the two are overlooked.

Some have tried to address this concern by pointing out various differences between the two theologians. Next, they either suggest (as Kent Reames has done) that those who find Hauerwas problematic need not also find Yoder problematic (or at least, not for the same reasons), or they suggest (as Douglas Harink has done) that the differences do not finally amount to any substantive disagreement, and we would do well not to feel the need to choose between them.[3] Therefore, though the space between Yoder and Hauerwas is certainly small relative to some others, it is worth examining some of what makes up this particular space. This kind of examination is rendered particularly difficult, though, by Hauerwas's own admission that "if there is in fact a difference—which may even amount

---

1. Debate with Paige Patterson at Southeastern Baptist Theological Seminary, September 18, 2002.

2. Carter, *Politics of the Cross*, 227.

3. See Reames, "Why Yoder Is Not Hauerwas," and Harink, "For or Against the Nations."

to a disagreement—between Yoder and me, no one should be tempted to side with me."[4]

Nevertheless, I do not think one needs to take sides in order to present important differences, or even disagreements.[5] Comparing these two theologians is not a simple matter of placing them side by side. Hauerwas draws so frequently and deeply from Yoder that we cannot merely point out where they overlap; rather we must specify the places where Hauerwas has adopted Yoder's thinking and those places where he has not. Because instances when Yoder engages Hauerwas are comparatively rare (and, even then, commonly in footnotes), I intend to look at ways that Hauerwas diverges from Yoder and not the other way around. By putting the matter this way, I do not wish to deny that Hauerwas may have influenced Yoder; indeed, he may have, even significantly. However, the influence has happened so strongly in the other direction that it warrants particular attention.

Much is often made of the suggestion that Yoder is essentially "For the Nations" and Hauerwas is essentially "Against the Nations," following their respective book titles. However, this invites a simplistic, reductionistic kind of characterization that we could well do without. It may certainly be the case that Hauerwas is more of a contrarian than Yoder, but such an observation does not say much that is particularly new or interesting. In what follows, I hope to engage this topic on another level. I will point out three closely related areas under the topic of the church's public witness where Hauerwas has intentionally not gone along with Yoder. These are the issues of Constantinianism in modernity, translatability, and the world's response to the church's witness.

Showing where Hauerwas's thinking departs from Yoder's may make some feel that this requires too much focus on Hauerwas and not enough on Yoder. This may indeed be true. Nevertheless, I hope that this will prove to be a productive strategy for treating two thinkers who are far more interested in taking on those who differ significantly from themselves. Their writings are often directed at different audiences, serve different purposes, and treat different topics. By attending to the ways that Hauerwas has not adopted every aspect of Yoder's program, I hope to

---

4. Hauerwas, foreword to *Politics of the Cross*, 10.

5. In what follows, I do, however, take sides. Where I side with Hauerwas, I do so despite Hauerwas's obvious false humility.

advance the ways we understand the contributions of both to the ongoing consideration and practice of the church's faithful witness in the world.

## CONSTANTINIANISM IN MODERNITY

Yoder and Hauerwas are certainly both opposed to Constantinianism, that is, the presumption that the church must take responsibility for making history come out right by aligning itself with state power. It was on this assumption that the church resorted to violence in the name of securing a future for itself and lost its critical edge and its distinctiveness. As a response, Yoder identifies four anti-Constantinian characteristics: 1) the assertion of "radical monotheism" against paganism and idolatry, 2) "missionary vigor derived from the conviction that a new messianic age is dawning," 3) "courage to stand as a minority in a hostile environment," and 4) "rejection of violence, based upon trust in God's protection."[6] It is commonly assumed—and there is certainly sufficient historical warrant to assume—that the first three items (assertion, missionary zeal, and courage) naturally imply the *opposite* of the fourth (rejection of violence). A version of this assumption says that all assertions (indeed all instances of speech) are necessarily violent, another that all missionary activity is necessarily an imposition. But Yoder, of course, carries on as though there is no tension. There is a paradox here according to the conventional wisdom that tells us that *patient and nonviolent* speech cannot also be *bold or zealous*. However, Yoder affirms all these things as constitutive of Christian witness. Let us therefore dwell on this theme for a moment.

The particular manifestation of Constantinianism called Christendom involved aligning the church with state power in a way that entailed leveling the citizenry of Europe: everyone was now a Christian by virtue of being a citizen of a Christian state or empire. The boundaries of Christendom coincided with the geographical and political boundaries of the empire. Religion became territorialized such that breaching those territories was seen as imperialistic and violent. In these conditions, then, refraining from proclaiming the gospel, on the assumption that it is no longer necessary, may *appear* to give expression to a rejection of imperi-

---

6. Yoder, *Royal Priesthood*, 247 n. 11. Yoder calls these marks "Jewish," because the anti-Constantinian heritage of the radical Reformation began to relate to the Jewish origins of Christianity differently on account of its disavowal of structures and institutions that, for instance, abstracted Christian faith from its particular roots.

alism. But this is not really non-Constantinian at all; it is still internal to a Constantinian way of thinking: "It is the application of Constantinian logic, and not necessarily a defense of human dignity, to posit that all Africans were 'happy' in their tribal religion until the missionaries came, every Tunisian satisfied with Islam . . . any more than every European is Christian."[7] Missionaries who violated human dignity by being culturally totalitarian are the other side of the same logic that takes the Christian mission to be inherently violent. A triumphalist Christianity was not too closely joined with Jesus but actually denied him in its contempt for neighbors. It was not too Christian, but not Christian enough.[8]

Even so, the apparent tension within the Christian witness is between *boldness and openness*. Are evangelical boldness and courage at odds with the vulnerability of the good news? Are the medium and the message held together in tension in this way? Where it is assumed that they are at odds, boldness is usually construed as a form of coercion, a construal Yoder challenges. Romand Coles summarizes Yoder's achievement as showing that faithful engagements are "at once evangelical and vulnerable. Or, evangelical in their vulnerability, and vulnerable in their evangelism."[9] The person of the Christian witness is more like a herald and less like an apologete since nothing the herald has can make others believe the message she bears: "The herald has no clout."[10] Bearing heraldic witness acknowledges that renunciation of force is part of the message. Gayle Gerber Koontz describes the action of the nonviolent herald:

> The Christian herald must remain doubly vulnerable—vulnerable because he or she is reporting a particular relative historical event that itself may or may not speak to others, and vulnerable because the herald has disavowed those affiliations which might convince others to join the Christian movement for the wrong reasons. Defenseless confession of faith can only be "distinguished" from the colonial or crusader truth claim if the herald's double vulnerability is clearly perceived and willingly affirmed.[11]

---

7. Yoder, *Royal Priesthood*, 255.
8. Ibid., 257.
9. Coles, "Wild Patience," 317.
10. Yoder, *Royal Priesthood*, 256.
11. Koontz, "Confessional Theology," 214.

Heralding the good news challenges the coercive logic of modern and postmodern discourse. The former assumes that the historical particularity of the Christian message is a liability (as Lessing thought when he famously identified an unbridgeable ditch between the accidental truths of history and the universal truths about God), and the latter accepts this liability when it disingenuously claims not to hold anything universally true. Both enshrine a Constantinian dualism between universality and particularity, though in differing ways.

In a slightly different form, the paradox of the Christian witness is also between *proclamation and dialogue.* Is not proclamation an imperialistic activity that one-sidedly tells others how it is? Is not dialogue, therefore, ruled out in advance in favor of a one-sided monologue? One problem arises when the difficulty is taken to involve "proclamation" in general, that is, as a style or mode of discourse, rather than proclamation of the lordship of Christ. It matters *what* is being proclaimed, and Yoder seeks to push the locus for authenticity of the witness—the testing place for its validity—out of the realm of abstract categories like "proclamation" and into the concreteness of visible Christian communities. This is because concepts that sit uneasily (or uncertainly) alongside each other, so long as they remain concepts, are sometimes able to coincide within actual communities.[12]

Yoder writes, "That gatheredness of the community is the point where the old language and the new challenges meet, where distinctiveness and commonality are tested, where kerygma and dialogue coincide, where renewed appeal to the biblical Jesus and renewed openness to tomorrow's world are not two things but one."[13] Even when the community takes a stand in terms of first principles, it nevertheless does so as a community already engaged in life with questions of value; that way of life is irreducible to any first principles that it formulates. "The life of the community is prior to all possible methodological distillations."[14] This

---

12. I say they are *sometimes able* to coincide within actual communities because there is no guarantee that they will; quite often, of course, they do not.

13. Yoder, *Royal Priesthood*, 253.

14. Yoder, "Walk and Word," 82. Also, "The church precedes the world epistemologically. We know more fully from Jesus Christ and in the context of the confessed faith than we know in other ways. The meaning and validity and limits of concepts like 'nature' or of 'science' are best seen not when looked at alone but in light of the confession of the lordship of Christ. The church precedes the world axiologically, in that the lordship of Christ is the center which must guide critical value choices, so that we may be called to subordi-

means that making recourse to an epistemology to do justificatory work on its own will always be a way of securing more ground for a particular intellectual subculture that would otherwise be much more vulnerable without it. The witness of the Christian community can risk nonpossessive discourse precisely because it speaks of a nonpossessive cross that was not vindicated by a stronger counterassertion, but by resurrection.[15]

Constantinianism, for Yoder, is an ever-present temptation, an approach that will always present itself when things are not going well for the witness of Christians, and when violence is at their disposal. That the Emperor Constantine has the dubious distinction of being associated with this temptation (which Yoder calls a heresy) may indicate that violence and coercion work so powerfully on the Christian conscience that even when Christianity ceases to be under explicit attack, we are inclined to try to make use of them alongside the Christian message. It is troubling to consider how quickly Christians with power make use of their power in ways that are nearly indistinguishable from the ways that they had formerly suffered from it at the hands of others.

If Constantinianism is for Yoder the primary threat to the church, then for Hauerwas the more persistent enemy is liberalism. Liberalism is the modern belief that reason admits to no tradition, that its justification and appeal require no grounding except in rationality *qua* rationality. It is therefore the reason of any clearly thinking person. In a word, it is universal. To be sure, Yoder was opposed to the Enlightenment concept of rationality too but not to the extent that Hauerwas is. Yet the difference is not simply a matter of degree, as though Yoder hates the Enlightenment but Hauerwas *really* hates the Enlightenment. Instead, Hauerwas identifies the Enlightenment with Constantinianism in a way that Yoder rarely, if ever, did.

---

nate or even to reject those values which contradict Jesus." Yoder, *Priestly Kingdom*, 11.

15. Sheldon Wolin speaks similarly of "fugitive democracy" as the indispensable mode of drawing on fragile commonalities in society. Wolin's notion is well summarized by William E. Connolly: "When [fugitive democracy] bursts onto the scene it extends old frontiers by drawing new groups, concerns, priorities, supports, or rights into them. Hence, democracy must not be governed too tightly by a prior set of moral principles, constitutional rules, corporate dictates, or normative codes. Democratic spontaneity encodes a measure of uncertainty and indeterminacy into the operative politics of the political." "Politics and Vision," 15–16. Fragile democracy resembles Yoder's hermeneutics of peoplehood in such a case as when Wolin states that "Democracy is an ephemeral phenomenon rather than a settled system" (*Politics and Vision*, 602).

Indeed, Yoder showed how the Constantinian temptation has taken different forms. Just because the church is no longer in the position to claim imperial dominance does not mean that it has not found new ways of being Constantinian; it has just done so through variations on the same theme. The social position of the church in liberal democracies has tended to be what Yoder calls "neo-neo-Constantinianism," that is, the stage of the original Constantinian project "where the church blesses her society (and particularly her own national society) without a formal identification therewith, or without religious rootage in the common people."[16] Since nations (at least outwardly) are no longer empires that attempt to be universal in their scope, and because these nations no longer rely on formal links with the church or ostensibly consider themselves to be Christian, the church cannot hold a Constantinian stance in the original sense. Nevertheless, the aims of a neo-neo-Constantinian strategy represent but a secularization of a Constantinian dream.[17]

The concern that fuels Hauerwas's polemic against liberalism, however, is not primarily rooted in the church's response to a modern ethos (although it includes this); it involves a thoroughgoing critique of the liberal project itself. Here he draws significantly on the work of philosopher Alasdair MacIntyre. Jeffrey Stout writes, "It is not clear how Hauerwas proposes to combine [the] anti-Constantinian narrative with the antimodern narrative he takes over from MacIntyre."[18] Nevertheless, it is clear that Hauerwas does combine them. From MacIntyre Hauerwas adopts the view that in the Enlightenment, theories of rationality suffered a great blow when they presumed to achieve universal significance by dispensing with the narrative framework that gave rationality coherence. As a consequence, moral reasoning no longer depended on systems of thought and practice. Therefore, in the modern period, not only did the church maintain a Constantinian stance, as Yoder contends, but also the world lost contact with the very conditions necessary for it to be virtuous.

---

16. Yoder, *Original Revolution*, 152.

17. Ibid., 151.

18. Stout, *Democracy and Tradition*, 153. This chapter was first written before Stout's book was published, and on the basis of a manuscript I cited with the author's permission. There is much to say now that Stout's book is in print, some of which I say in the following chapter.

For Hauerwas, the false universalism of liberalism is but a form of Constantinianism. He writes, "Christian adherence to foundationalist epistemologies—that is, the kind of position we find exemplified in thinkers such as Kant—was commensurate with social strategies of Christendom," and "I am not asking the church to withdraw, but rather to give up the presumptions of Constantinian power, particularly when those take the form of liberal universalism."[19] This means that a church that rejects the strategies of Christendom cannot help but find itself incommensurate with liberalism. This is because both Christendom and liberalism rely on false universals.

It is important to note that Yoder is not committed to incommensurability between the church and the world as Hauerwas is. This is because he does not connect the project of Christendom with the project of the Enlightenment as Hauerwas does, even though he is often vigorously critical of both. Hauerwas represents, therefore, a combination of Yoder and MacIntyre, in his notion of incommensurability. Indeed he notes, "It is probably a sign of the unusual times in which we live that I can be at once influenced by Alasdair MacIntyre and John Howard Yoder without feeling a deep sense of contradiction."[20] These unusual times, no doubt, involve the temptation toward absolutizing Christian claims to power over history, on the grounds that the dominant forms of rationality make such absolutizing not only possible but in some sense inevitable.

Stout observes this when he writes, "One cannot stand in a church conceived in Yoder's terms, while describing the world surrounding it in the way MacIntyre describes liberal society, without implicitly adopting a stance that is rigidly dualistic."[21] However, saying that the church and the world are incommensurate with one another is not necessarily the same as dualism if by dualism we mean some kind of ontological separation. Ontologically, the church and the world are both under the lordship of Christ and have been given the same possibilities. Hauerwas follows Yoder in maintaining that if there is a duality, it is not over the domain of Christ's lordship but over agency: "between the basic personal postures of men, some of whom confess and others of whom do not confess that

---

19. Hauerwas, *After Christendom?* 15, 18.
20. Ibid., 9.
21. Stout, *Democracy and Tradition*, 149.

Jesus Christ is Lord."[22] There may be a descriptive dualism but not an ontological one or, better, not a necessary dualism but a contingent one.[23]

In the same way, incommensurability is not a way of talking about the church's relationship to the world at all times and places. For example, Constantine did not become Constantinian because he shared liberal presuppositions about universal reason, but because he got wrong "the course of history, its direction and meaningfulness."[24] In the modern period, the Constantinian temptation was legitimated in a new way; its legitimation sanctioned the support of nation-states since the church no longer held political power as the church. When it held power, its power was due only to its close affiliation to the nation-state. In this situation, as long as the church confronts the epistemological assumptions of liberalism, which make inevitable a demand that the church either adopt a Constantinian social strategy or admit irrelevance, it cannot help but exist incommensurably with such a world.

Of course, this state of affairs has potentially been reshaped by pluralist and relativist critiques. Hauerwas suggests that a possible form of the church's witness might involve being "tactical allies of the pluralism/relativist questioning of the secular orthodoxies that promise certainty through coercion" but warns against exalting relativism on its own terms.[25] Relativism may make a useful partner in the struggle against the Enlightenment. In suggesting this strategy, Hauerwas deliberately follows Yoder's use of the term "tactical allies" from Yoder's essay, "But We Do See Jesus."[26] Still, it is telling that Hauerwas does not take up Yoder's suggestion that we might ally ourselves even with the Enlightenment. This is the one thing that Christians have been more than willing to do, and so, it could be argued, the church is in no position to make an alliance with such a seductive enemy. Certainly too much could be made of this point, especially since it argues from silence (i.e., from what Hauerwas does *not* say), and both theologians have written far too much to warrant an argu-

---

22. Yoder, *Original Revolution*, 116. See also Hauerwas, "Messianic Pacifism," 32.

23. Yoder characterized some Mennonite theology, such as Hershberger's, as holding an ontological dualism in which Christians live by nonviolence and the state lives by violence. Yoder, *Nevertheless*, 113.

24. Yoder, *Original Revolution*, 148.

25. Hauerwas, *With the Grain of the Universe*, 224–25

26. Yoder, *Priestly Kingdom*, 61.

ment from silence. Yet it is instructive in a paradigmatic way of a subtle but real difference between these two theologians.

For one, Yoder does not want to reject some of the fruits of modern liberalism to the extent that Hauerwas wants. He is sympathetic to a "soft pluralism." He writes, "From the Gospel perspective, modern pluralism is not a setback but a providential occasion for clarification."[27] He goes on to suggest that pluralism can make life more livable for minority voices and so is preferable to the alternatives. Of course, it is a form of Constantinianism when we begin to ask what the best form of government is,[28] but the state is under divine lordship to maintain order so that the church can bear witness to a new sociality.[29]

But Hauerwas does not think that what we have should be called pluralism since it has produced enormously conformist consumers in a capitalist economy.[30] This conformity is, in some sense, achieved in the name of pluralism, that is, under the illusion of free choice. Following Nicholas Boyle, Hauerwas is suspicious of suggestions that the global expression of so-called pluralism may, in fact, provide a better ethos for the church. Indeed, it may be just as tempting, "For the new order is a kind of universality whose ambition is to rule minds and bodies just as nations did so effectively in the past."[31]

Even worse, the language of pluralism admits to a variety of so-called postmodern discourse that is still essentially modern. Hauerwas says that he is not convinced that "postmodernism, either as an intellectual position or as a cultural style, is post-anything."[32] Instead, it is the "bastard offspring" of modernism to the extent that it continues to presuppose an ahistorical viewpoint based on the false presumption of personal liberty.[33] The language of pluralism relies on a notion of relativism that is still a modern description.

Even though Yoder wants to maintain pluralism, he reminds Stout that the assumption that "relativism is something recent and threaten-

---

27. Yoder, "Meaning after Babble," 135.
28. Yoder, *Priestly Kingdom*, 154.
29. See Weaver, "After Politics," 663.
30. See Hauerwas, *After Christendom?* 97–98.
31. Hauerwas, *A Better Hope*, 45.
32. Ibid., 37.
33. Ibid., 38.

ing, rests upon nostalgia for a prior epoch of Establishment. There never was an homogeneous moral language; it only seemed that there was because the other voices were not heard."[34] The charge of relativism, like the charge of sectarianism, is only a version of the modernist ethos that makes notions like relativism and sectarianism inevitable. Relativism is the language that postmodernists revert to in a way that betrays their modernist commitments. But if objectivism is false, it is not false because relativism is true, but because neither objectivism nor relativism has merit as a distinct category. But for Yoder, the hearing of the unheard voices, so crucial to dismantling the false universalism of modernity, is accomplished by a modern pluralism that Hauerwas essentially rejects on the grounds that even within said pluralism such minority voices are not given opportunity to speak so much as they are made to think that they have relatively little to say. With Yoder, Hauerwas rejects the language of relativism as essentially modern, but with MacIntyre he suspects that the language of pluralism is too.

I have been trying to show that Yoder and Hauerwas conceive of Constantinianism's modern expression somewhat differently. It should not be surprising that, comparatively, Hauerwas rarely even uses the term "Constantinian," instead preferring to name liberalism on its own. This owes to Hauerwas's particular combination of MacIntyre's identification of liberalism with the Christendom fantasy. Put simply (and at the risk of oversimplification), when it comes to Constantinianism and liberalism, the difference between Yoder and Hauerwas is MacIntyre.

## TRANSLATABILITY

Much of Yoder's work was devoted to articulating how the church could be involved in more secular peace movements and work for justice and so forth in the public arena. Yoder's first and most influential suggestion in this regard came in his book *The Christian Witness to the State*.[35] There Yoder employs the concept of "middle axioms," which was a popular concept in ecumenical circles at the time. By it he meant that the church should employ ways of addressing specific actions of the state, not in the native language of the church but in the language of the state. Christians,

---

34. Yoder, "Meaning after Babble," 134–35.
35. Yoder, *Christian Witness to the State*.

therefore, witness to the state by selectively calling the state to live up to the state's own highest ideals and stated principles.

Making these kinds of appeals to the state would then involve the ad hoc deployment of Christian norms formulated in "pagan terms" such as, Yoder suggests, liberty, equality, fraternity, education, democracy, and human rights.[36] The pagan terms do not have an existence of their own but have a temporary usefulness to the Christian, who knows that "the ultimate ground for their validity is the love of Christ."[37] As Alain Epp Weaver comments, "No metaphysical value is ascribed to the middle axioms outside of Christ."[38]

A significant difference arises here between Yoder and Hauerwas, because Hauerwas has "a number of theological and philosophical misgivings about the very idea of translation."[39] Of course, Hauerwas had in mind bigger offenders than Yoder (most notably James Gustafson) when he expressed his misgivings. Nevertheless, one suspects that, for him, middle axioms come too close to the kind of Enlightenment project that produced the accommodationist church in America. But perhaps more important, the idea of translation as a means to communicate is philosophically problematic.

Following Ludwig Wittgenstein, Hauerwas asserts that language is intelligible only within determinate settings (or linguistic communities) that arise from shared skills and practices.[40] Intelligibility is not intrinsic to language or even to a particular message, but depends on the recipient's being able to understand what is said as communication, based on using these skills and practices. In other words, much of what we typically refer to as translation is really the speaking of a second message. To speak in a different context and have the speech count as communication requires training in the second form of life and learning to speak that language. This is not translation, since the bearer of meaningful utterance is not semantic but communal in nature. Put differently, the world cannot know

---

36. Ibid., 73.
37. Ibid.
38. Weaver "After Politics," 670.
39. Hauerwas, *Wilderness Wanderings*, 3.
40. See Kallenberg, *Ethics as Grammar*, 119–33. The language of linguistic communities is adopted from Stanley Fish and is prominent in Hauerwas, *Unleashing the Scripture*.

what Christians might mean by "human rights" without entering into worship.

Since the language of liberalism, in Hauerwas's words, "has been and is the speech that dominates our lives,"[41] the church is challenged to inhabit an alternative speech community that takes seriously the inability to separate language from the world. Pagan terms cannot help but communicate pagan meaning even when Christians use them.[42] Even when intended as a translation of *agape*, the language of liberty does not challenge the presumption that the freedom of the individual is primary, a notion incompatible with God's love. Nevertheless, it would be a mistake to assume that the problem lies with words themselves, as if dictionaries could be divided into lists of pagan words and Christian words. There is nothing particularly sacred about *agape* since surely, as a word, it had meaning before Christians started using it. What is pagan, therefore, is not the term but the horizon of meaning that a people give to it through how they use it. Christian training in Christian speech is not adoption of a new vocabulary but learning how to speak the new life that Christ has made possible in his death and resurrection. This means that even pagan terms can be redeemed, but not apart from the redemption of the people who use them. To be sure, this cannot mean that Christians ought not speak to the world, but only that in doing so, Christians never seek to convey information through their proclamation of the good news, but seek to extend an invitation to inhabit a new way of life that makes possible a new way of speaking. Christians have the confidence that the gospel can be proclaimed throughout the world, but such confidence does not come through beliefs about the translation of words or concepts, but through the promise of God to meet the witness of Christians as it embodies the words it speaks. For Hauerwas, Christian speech resists translation not only on account of the material content of Christian convictions—although this is true—but it resists translation primarily because the very idea of translation is spurious.[43]

---

41. Hauerwas, "Failure of Communication," 231.

42. But this is not *all* that they do.

43. Gary Dorrien recounts an episode when Ronald Sider challenged Hauerwas at a conference on Niebuhr to say that Christians ought to be concerned with the right ordering of the world, on the basis of biblical claims about the kingdom of God and on the basis of an imperative for seeking positive social change. Dorrien asks how Hauerwas can "deny that following Christ has something to do with caring about the right ordering

The difference with Yoder is significant but subtle. Yoder is not the best representative of the position that Hauerwas argues against. After all, middle axioms, for Yoder, are not perfect translations, and some translations are not defensible. He laments, for example, the "ease with which the word 'freedom' replaces the name 'Jesus'" among oppressed peoples who sing of liberation. The problem is not that a translation has happened, but instead that we need to ask "whether the word 'freedom,' with all the freight of meaning which it has come to have in the contemporary movement, is big enough and true enough to say everything that the name of Jesus must mean."[44]

Nevertheless, in the concept of middle axioms, Yoder relied on the ability of Christians to translate their convictions into the language used by the state. The state is thus called to approximate Christian norms more closely even though the translated message need not have recourse to the language of those norms in their biblical and traditional formulations.

Michael Cartwright correctly observes that over time Yoder dropped the language of middle axioms, although he never specifically repudiated it as a notion.[45] What is clear, however, is that Yoder began increasingly to focus the language of witness on the church side of the church/world distinction. It is an open question whether middle axioms dropped out of his vocabulary and whether the role of translatability in political witness was diminished due to misgivings over translatability or for some other reason. Yoder's essay "The Christian Case for Democracy," for example, clearly relies on a kind of translation across three "semantic frames": how the faith community speaks internally, how it speaks to the nations, and

---

of the world when the New Testament repeatedly proclaims that it does?

"'Because when people say that, they always become Constantinian,' Hauerwas immediately replied. 'They want you to play the game of responsibility. Aha, they say, you're not being responsible! But, because of Niebuhr, responsibility carries a whole set of presumptions that I don't want to accept'" (Dorrien, *Soul in Society*, 358).

Dorrien is critical of this, partly because he sees Hauerwas as having accepted a Niebuhrian premise that he should really deny, namely, that the ethics of the kingdom is necessarily at odds with justice (and hence responsibility). Yoder also found it necessary to avoid, clarify, or reject language of responsibility (and effectiveness), depending on who he was talking to. I think Dorrien is mistaken to think that this involves an acceptance of Niebuhr; instead, it involves an awareness of how pervasive the Niebuhrian assumption is. Put differently, the demands of nonviolence cannot help but be distorted or entirely lost when rendered in certain language.

44. Yoder, *For the Nations*, 121.
45. Cartwright, "Radical Reform," 17.

how the nations speak on their own terms.[46] Here it could be argued that Yoder essentially retains the notion of middle axioms but drops the terminology.

In several essays and eventually in the book *Body Politics*, Yoder sets forth what appears to be his own improvement to the previous notion of "middle axioms," namely, a set of "five practices of the Christian community before the watching world."[47] The advantage of the practices of *Body Politics* over middle axioms lies in the fact that the practices are meant to be *constitutive* of the church's very existence; they are a part of what the church *is* rather than what the church *does*. Of course, by definition, a practice is something that is done, but in the case of the particular practices that Yoder suggests, he does not intend for us to imagine the church even existing apart from these kinds of practices. Put simply, the church does not do what it does because the world is watching, but because it is called to faithfulness. The substance of Yoder's approach here derives from the acknowledgement that worship and ethics are not, in the end, separable.

Yet "each of these practices can function as a paradigm for ways in which other social groups might operate" since "they are accessible to the public. People who do not share the faith or join the community can learn from them."[48] This way of putting "witness" is much closer to Hauerwas's language than was the language of middle axioms.

Even though he is careful to indicate that these five practices are meant to be crucial to the life of the church, Yoder has in mind that they also cannot help but witness to the world. He notes that in addition to being a form of the church's faithfulness to God, a practice "at the same time offers a paradigm for the life of the larger society."[49] For example, in the Eucharist we find the normative Christian affirmation that disciples break bread together. This involves feeding the hungry and all eating in turn regardless of rank or class. For Yoder, a churchly practice has an identifiable, social dimension that witnesses to the world and "is a

---

46. Yoder, *Priestly Kingdom*, 160–61. Also "It is sufficient to be aware of the relativity of our linguistic rulings to be able to translate from one frame to the other" (ibid., 164).

47. This is the subtitle to Yoder, *Body Politics*.

48. Yoder, *Royal Priesthood*, 369.

49. Yoder, *Body Politics*, x.

paradigm, not only for soup kitchens and hospitality houses, but also for social security and negative income tax."[50]

However, by focusing on practices, Yoder does not give up entirely on the project of translation. He insists that the practices *are* translatable because they are not "religious" activities but "are by nature 'lay' or 'public' phenomena."[51] Perhaps with Hauerwas in mind, Yoder addresses the concern over the use of mediating language:

> Some have warned me that it is dangerous to borrow such worldly words as "egalitarian" or "freedom" since those concepts are not only hard to define but are the property of the liberal establishment, which is an oppressive elite. These friends are right in thus warning me. If I were to think that those contemporary terms have a univocal normative meaning, and if I were proposing that they simply be "baptized," I should have sold out. But those warning friends are wrong if they suggest that some other, less liberal words (for example "virtue," "narrative," "community") would be safer from abuse. The right corrective is not to seek fail-safe words never yet corrupted but rather to renew daily the action of preempting the extant vocabulary, rendering every creature subject to God's rule in Christ. What is needed is to surface the criteria whereby we can tell whether, in the appropriation of each new language, the meaning of Jesus is authentically reenacted or abandoned.[52]

Here Yoder comes close to addressing Hauerwas's philosophical misgivings about translatability. He is making one of two possible moves. On the one hand, Yoder may be primarily defending the integrity of practices and language. "Preempting the extant vocabulary" might take the form of inhabiting "liberal" words with new practices, and the "criteria" he has in mind for determining whether a language is true to Jesus are themselves practices. On the other hand, Yoder may be primarily defending the practice of translation where practices make the translation authentic. So when the church speaks about freedom, for example, and knows that it means something different from the liberal meaning, its truthful living supports its redeemed use.[53]

50. Yoder, *Royal Priesthood*, 370.
51. Ibid.
52. Ibid. See also Yoder, *Body Politics*, 72.
53. I think this is most likely. The kind of mediation enacted by the practices, Yoder

In either case, Yoder is clearly onto a project quite different from middle axioms and, in significant respects, closer to Hauerwas. However Yoder intends to support the witnessing power of churchly practices, he does not intend to suggest that the state be called to live up to its own highest stated ideals. Instead the church, as part of its internal worship life, is of service to the world. It suggests possibilities that apart from the presence of an alternative community of belief, the world could not know. These possibilities are normative not only for the church but for the whole world since Jesus is Lord over all.

## THE WORLD'S RESPONSE TO THE CHURCH'S WITNESS

For both Yoder and Hauerwas, the witness of the church is primarily a matter of being a visible, real, alternative community of belief in a world of unbelief.[54] This community lives as though the kingdom has come in Jesus Christ and so is equipped to live in a new way.[55] Therefore, the church is a model to the world of what has been made possible since Jesus is Lord over the whole world. The two theologians, however, differ over the kind of response to witness that the church can normally expect from the world. In this, they differ quite apart from the issue of translation. Yoder is much more optimistic about the world's response. The new possibilities made real in the life of the church for the wider society are made explicit in practices that do not necessarily require translation, as we have seen.

---

says, "is not a mental or verbal operation of translation or conceptual bridging, but rather the concrete historical presence, among their neighbors, of believers who for Jesus's sake do ordinary social things differently" (*Body Politics*, 75). Moreover, Yoder rejects Zwinglianism, in which a practice (say, baptism) is a mere *sign* that "reduces symbolic action to an acted-out message, which can be equally well translated into words" (ibid., 33). I take this to mean that when the church makes use of vocabulary such as "egalitarian," it has not made a translation but has improvised linguistically. But Yoder is not always consistent, such as when he goes on to conclude that "All five of the practices we have been reviewing can be spoken of in social process terms. They can be translated into non-religious terms" (ibid., 71–72). To which I want to ask, "without remainder?" I admit that I simply do not know how to reconcile these statements.

54. Yoder, *Original Revolution*, 116. This is the thesis of Hauerwas and Willimon, *Resident Aliens*.

55. "As though," of course, is a problematic construction since the knowledge of the kingdom is not a postulate on the basis of which the church enacts its common life, but is the very condition of possibility for that life.

According to Hauerwas, however, the world may well convert as a result of the church's witness, but such witness is more likely to yield contempt than awe. The watching world is more likely to reject the church's witness than to learn from it. This is because the truthfulness of the church's witness runs so contrary to the world that the world will not immediately recognize it as true. There is nothing that *necessarily* prevents anyone from learning from Christian practices, and Yoder was right to think we should not be surprised when such learning takes place.[56] Still, Yoder's account of practices (such as his insistence that there is nothing mysterious about the Lord's Supper) may be insufficiently complex.[57] A sacramental logic is only one form of the theo-logic necessary to make Christian practices intelligible, since the narrative enacted by a practice (such as the kind of narrative remembrance the Eucharist names) is precisely what allows the practice to be sustained even when no one takes notice.[58] In the event that the church's witness *is* met with conversion, it is the result of a crisis. The world may learn from the church's refusal to live according to violence, for example, but not without radical discontinuity with the world's whole public program that seems to require violence. Here Hauerwas adopts MacIntyre's notion of an epistemological crisis.

According to MacIntyre, incommensurable traditions are domains that cannot simultaneously have purchase on the human agent or community, and the movement from one to the other requires an epistemological crisis.[59] Hauerwas notes that witness is disruptive: "That Christians are first and foremost called to be witnesses by necessity creates epistemological crises for those who do not worship the God of Jesus Christ."[60] The church witnesses to the truth about the way that the world has been

---

56. A forthcoming posthumous collection of Yoder's essays, *The War of the Lamb*, explicitly takes up this theme and enlarges it by including the question of effectiveness: even though Christian nonviolence does not promise to be effective, to convert anyone, to prevent one from getting killed, sometimes it actually has some of these effects. How, Yoder asks, are we to understand this contingent relation?

57. Yoder, *Body Politics*, chapter 2. Nevertheless, Yoder claims, "they are actions of God, in and with, through and under what men and women do" (ibid., 72–73). He therefore argues that "sacrament" ought to be acceptable nomenclature even among those who have rejected it, especially identifying the free-church tradition, which has preferred to talk about "ordinances," disabusing anything "magical" or "superstitious" in them. I admit to feeling as though Yoder underestimates the best of higher liturgical traditions.

58. I am grateful to conversations with Justin Ashworth on this topic.

59. See MacIntyre, "Epistemological Crises."

60. Hauerwas, *Sanctify Them in the Truth*, 187.

made new on account of the cross and resurrection. The problem is that the world does not know that the world as it appears is not the way things really are. This is because the appearance of the world as unredeemed marks what it means for those who see the world that way to be called "world." "World" in this sense is Christian nomenclature. By living according to the new age, the church in its witness challenges the belief that the world is in possession of ultimate reality. This throws the one who does not believe into an epistemological crisis that calls into question the narrative that gives rise to the unquestioned assumption about the reality of the world. Hauerwas notes that a "new narrative is required for the resolution of an epistemological crisis. Such a narrative must enable the agent to understand both how they could have intelligibly held their former beliefs and how they may have been misled by them."[61] Conversion, then, is fitting one's life into the narrative that resolves the crisis.

Of course, putting the matter this way is far too simplistic insofar as it suggests that an epistemological crisis is followed by a dramatic and immediate resolution. Hauerwas follows MacIntyre in arguing that traditions may for a long period of time coexist without resolving conflict, which is to say, without the recognition that a crisis exists.[62] Hauerwas draws attention to war as the necessary result when "traditions are unable to recognize the crises they create for each other."[63]

Similarly, learning to see one's life in the ongoing narrative of Jesus and of the church is a lifelong process of learning the reality of what was accomplished in baptism. This is also more generally true of the church's witness to the world. Without the presence of the church as an alternative community that lives in a way newly made possible in Christ, the world, in Hauerwas's words, "cannot know that it is the world."[64] It cannot know that all along it has been assuming that the world is the full extent of all possibilities unless an alternative possibility exists to challenge that assumption.

Even though much of the language of the "alternative community" is Yoder's, Yoder does not see witness as involving much of a crisis. This is because, for him, the practical rationality of the church is commensurate with that of the world. The world is in need only of a truthful message

61. Ibid., 186.
62. Ibid., 187.
63. Ibid.
64. Hauerwas and Willimon, *Resident Aliens*, 94.

proclaimed and witnessed with integrity. With Hauerwas, Yoder maintains that the church's witness is a witness about the way the world really is. The difference is that according to Hauerwas, the world cannot readily recognize the world as it is, apart from adopting the very practices of worship and so forth that allow for the acknowledgement that the material content of the church's witness might, in fact, be true.

It should be clear that the epistemological crisis correlates with Hauerwas's views on translatability and incommensurability. Epistemological crisis is the means by which one tradition adopts another or, better, converts from one to the other. There is no significant translation of the Christian message but instead the display of the effective causes for an epistemological crisis, should the world turn and believe. Put differently, the practices of Christian worship and service are for Yoder the carriers of the message and, at times, the message itself, whereas for Hauerwas such practices are also the means by which the practitioner comes to see the truthfulness and reality of the message.[65]

## CONCLUSION

Noting that Yoder is "For the Nations" and Hauerwas is "Against the Nations" is not to say much on its own. Both theologians deserve much more attention than that unfortunate characterization.[66] Certainly there

65. It will be clear that I think Hauerwas offers a better account in this regard. For example, following New Testament baptismal formulae, Yoder speaks about baptism in terms of relativizing status, whether it relates to slavery, gender, or class. See Yoder, "Sacrament as Social Process," 38–39. Yoder claims that the world may look on and learn something about egalitarianism. But I am not convinced that we can expect anyone to conclude that the relativization of status that baptism enacts is a "good thing," a better way to be in the world, or an improved form of sociality apart from actually being baptized. Such a question cannot be answered in the abstract but will need to be investigated historically. Surely martyrs have not always been killed because their killers have misunderstood Christianity; often their killers have understood it all too well, and it provoked their hostility.

66. Yoder himself thought the characterization of his own position as "against the nations" is mistaken, though he admits that the essays in *The Royal Priesthood* were chosen by editor Michael Cartwright perhaps along the lines of this vision. See *For the Nations*, 6. In parallel fashion, Hauerwas attempts to clarify the task of his career when he describes the essays in *A Better Hope*: "Christians cannot afford to let ourselves be defined by what we are against. Whatever or whomever we are against, we are so only because God has given us so much to be for. *A Better Hope* is my attempt to make the 'for' more determinative than the 'against.' Of course I should like to think that books like *After Christendom?* and *Against the Nations*, polemical though they may be, are so only because of what I

are differences; there may in fact be disagreements. The differences I have noted between Yoder and Hauerwas may be subtle, but they are real. They bear on the nature of the church, the world, and the church's witness to the world.

But what are we to make of these differences? It is not at all clear to me whether a Mennonite needs Wittgenstein (or MacIntyre) as much as does a Methodist graduate of Yale. Hauerwas's Yale mistook particularity for universality in a way that the Mennonite world was never privileged to do. Put more contentiously, maybe Mennonites do not need a prophet against liberalism as badly as the rest of us do.[67] I suspect this is a reason that only a John Howard Yoder could write against methodologism as effortlessly as he did; he knew what most of us do not, namely, a "concrete social genuineness of the community's reasoning together in the Spirit."[68]

If we insist on making a distinction between being for or against the nations, we do so at the expense of more thoughtful attention to the way of God in the world. Perhaps Yoder himself said it best:

> For the people of God to be over against the world at those points where "the world" is defined by its rebellion against God and for us to be in, with and for the world, as anticipation of the shape of redemption, are not alternative strategies. We are not free to choose between them, depending on whether our tastes are more "catholic" or more "baptist," or depending on whether we think the times are friendly just now or not. Each dimension of our stance is the prerequisite for the validity of the other. A church that is not "against the world" in fundamental ways has nothing worth saying to and for the world. Conversion and separation are not the way to become otherworldly; they are the only way to be present, relevantly and redemptively, in the midst of things.[69]

---

have been for" (*A Better Hope*, 9). Also, in a very interesting essay in *Disruptive Grace*, George Hunsinger perhaps overstates a critique of Yoder's reading of Barth, but, even so, Hunsinger paints Yoder as a thinker for whom the *against* is more determinative than the *for*, whereas for Barth, "[I]t is only because the church is for the world that it must be against it" (122). I conclude the present chapter with a quotation from Yoder that says essentially the same thing. I am not convinced that Barth, Yoder, and Hauerwas are really very different in this regard.

67. I interpret James McClendon as claiming that Hauerwas is a prophet against liberalism in McClendon, Review of *Christian Existence Today*, 427.

68. Yoder, "Walk and Word," 87.

69. Yoder, *Body Politics*, 78.

CHAPTER 3

## Democracy Beyond Democracy

A number of contemporary ethical debates appear to have foreclosed on some crucial questions: Is there any possibility for moral discourse, given pluralism? Are the available modes of discourse—such as democracy—true vehicles for conversation or just disguised ways of conceding to one or more groups? Princeton University professor of religion Jeffrey Stout, in refusing to accept the finality of the answers given to these and related questions, has produced a book important by any reckoning. *Democracy and Tradition* will significantly advance the discussion about liberalism and democracy, particularly among those who are weary of these notions. At its strongest, Stout's case is refreshing because he sets forth a democracy with some teeth to it—it is not simply a "notion" but a robust tradition in its own right that no one ought to give up on. And Stout is not content to leave descriptions of democracy to lesser storytellers, whom he accuses of distorting the historical narrative and of rhetorically privileging their own positions. In this mission, Stout's main targets are three current critics of liberalism who represent what he calls "new traditionalism": John Milbank, Alasdair MacIntyre, and Stanley Hauerwas.

Stout positions himself as a middle way between, on the one hand, liberals who think that democracy works best either if all mention of religion is purged from discussion (e.g., Richard Rorty) or if religion is confined simply to contractarian schemes (e.g., John Rawls), and, on the other hand, those whom he takes to have rejected this form of democracy in favor of distinctive religious and virtuous traditions (i.e., the new traditionalists). In doing this, he is claiming to be in the good dialectical company of Hegel and American pragmatism. Stout wants religious believers to join in constructive, democratic conversation, and he impressively exemplifies this kind of conversation through engagement with his interlocutors. Among the threats to this kind of conversation is rhetorical excess, which caricatures, shortcuts by labeling, and overwhelms with grandiose diagnoses and pronouncements—all charges Stout pins on the new traditionalists to varying degrees.

Yet even if it is sometimes greatly overstated, Stout thinks there *is* some truth to the case that the new traditionalists make against liberalism. He agrees with them that forms of democratic exchange that require contributions to be dispossessed of their particular (religious, ethnic, ideological) content are incoherent and cannot be truly democratic. For Rawls, the particularity of belief belongs in the private realm of homes and churches but does not qualify for public discussion, which must rely on what can be taken for granted by everybody involved. While Stout thinks there may be *pragmatic* reasons for speaking on the level of what can be taken for granted in a pluralistic setting, this does not mean that religious reasons are to be dismissed out of hand.

Even so, Stout has not managed successfully to distance himself from Rawls as much as he thinks. He continues the problematic assumption of a public/private distinction in a way that is surprising, given what he says elsewhere. For example, his characterization of a "colloquy of coreligionists" as belonging to the private realm is inconsistent with what he wants to say about Martin Luther King Jr.'s public contribution to democratic discourse since, after all, King started a revolution in so-called private settings—with sermons in southern churches. This dichotomy perpetuates the division between "politics" and "religion" at the heart of liberalism, and Stout finally is unable to overcome it. He rightly discards Rawls's description of how to speak in public but continues to accept Rawls's description of what counts as the public sphere. Stout is wrong here: religious beliefs are not simply *reasons* or *presuppositions* that undergird political practice; Christianity is its own politics, which can look only like withdrawal when it is depoliticized through prior Rawlsian assumptions about what it means to be "political."

Stanley Hauerwas, in a postscript to his book *Performing the Faith: Bonhoeffer and the Practice of Nonviolence*, has responded quite sympathetically to Stout. He considers it an extraordinary act of goodwill that Stout "thinks theology matters."[1] Yet it is curious that Hauerwas does not engage with Stout ecclesiologically. Hauerwas is known for insisting

---

1. Hauerwas, *Performing the Faith*, 217.

that the church be the church: that is, a political body in its own right. A church that waits until it hears from its weakest members before acting and does not privilege the rules of engagement in favor of particular outcomes may certainly look like democracy. But it is much more than that: it is actually the practice of being Christian together. The church finds that it can imagine a "democracy" that is more democratic than the democracy of liberal political legitimation too easily taken for granted in American life.

In telling the story of liberal democracy, Stout attempts to renarrate the emergence of "the secular." He disagrees with Milbank's claim that secular*ism* is ideological and instead suggests a modest version of secular*ization*, the empirical reality of religious and other pluralisms that characterize modern society and its discussions of various goods. Addressing this pluralistic state of affairs, then, is not a matter of accepting a doctrine but of pragmatically negotiating how to speak in contexts where one cannot assume that others will see things in the same way.

Stout renarrates as he does because he believes that if he can show that the new traditionalists are wrong about liberal democracy, they will have to accept it. Thus, the book's argument is primarily a defense of liberal democracy that seeks to show, not only that liberal democracy is itself a tradition, but also that it can admit to being a tradition, without contradiction. Stout's target is mostly MacIntyre's view that liberalism has abandoned the traditions necessary for the transmission of virtues over time by unseating the political centrality of virtuous communities in exchange for the primacy of traditionless individuals. Consequently, for MacIntyre, inheritors of liberalism are doomed to moral incoherence, attempting to negotiate diverse "virtues" detached from the communal structures that formerly produced the kinds of virtuous people who actually gave content to those virtues. Stout thinks MacIntyre's account "tells a largely false story," and that liberal democracy really entails its own particular piety as part of its intellectual tradition.[2] Thinkers like Emerson and Whitman exemplify this liberal piety as members of a distinctive democratic tradition.

But Stout's strategy, for all it succeeds in doing, is seriously flawed in one major respect. For Milbank and Hauerwas, at least, what is most interesting is not why they *reject* liberalism but what they *affirm* and pro-

---

2. Stout, *Democracy and Tradition*, 12.

mote instead. The problem is not so much that liberal democracy rests on an untenable rendering of social contracts and excessive restrictions on what counts as legitimate expression; or that liberal democracy is not a tradition (even MacIntyre admits that it is). Rather the problem is that liberal democracy's piety is insufficiently imaginative. It does not claim *too much*, but it is content to settle for *too little*, given the possibilities for human community that Christians affirm God makes available now through the future world of the kingdom come and coming. By focusing on Milbank's history of secularism and Hauerwas's negative critiques of liberalism, Stout misses this point and so inadequately addresses the positive, radical politics in their thought (though he does wish Milbank would say more about Christian socialism and Hauerwas would say more about Dorothy Day).

Stout thinks the Hauerwas of the seventies was on the right track with character and narrative ethics but got derailed through an appropriation of John Howard Yoder and MacIntyre in the early eighties. And though Stout is not interested in directly engaging Yoder, he would have done better to consider with greater depth the difference Yoder makes to this debate. Bearing witness to God's kingdom come and coming may mean that Christians decide, from time to time and in varying degrees, to take part in democratic institutions and processes in the ways that Stout advocates. The problem is not that there is a rigid church/world dualism; the problem is rather how Christians are to articulate our service in the world without confusing the church with America—something that occupied Yoder (and that occupies Hauerwas) considerably.

By not making a theological rebuttal of his own, Stout seems to distort the theological ways in which Hauerwas proceeds in the dualisms (church/world, modern/antimodern) that Stout critiques. Stout can only "win" if he can adequately respond to what he takes to be the nontheological arguments he opposes. But this is a problem for Stout, since it means he must recast Hauerwas's critique of liberalism and Milbank's genealogy of secularism in nontheological terms. In doing so, he wrongly assumes that his opponents are equipped with theological "reasons" rather than with an alternative theological description of our shared world. This is a function of Stout's own inability to imagine the political possibilities Christianity entails.

Stout worries that the critiques the new traditionalists offer against modernity tend to be overly bleak. In turn, critics like Hauerwas have no choice but to become antimodern or premodern. With reference to Orwell, Stout says that some people think "half a loaf is the same as no bread."[3] But this is why it matters that Christian politics is, in a sense, all about bread—half a loaf does not indicate scarcity but that what has been broken is shared, because the bread of life is really in abundance. The difference is in the Christian's ability to imagine possibilities otherwise unthinkable, because the Christian describes the world differently. If Christians are tempted to doubt the full extent of modernity's professed possibilities, it is not from despair, but hope. In this regard, it is unclear whether Stout can point to positive democratic practices in the same way that Christians can point to the Eucharist and say, "This is politics."

Will the new traditionalists influence their readers to be second-generation conservatives who wrongly confuse being traditional with being radical, as Stout fears? Is it true that for Christians who reject liberalism, Pat Robertson is right around the corner? Perhaps only if we despair. Hauerwas is afraid that an inordinate confidence in democracy leads to Reinhold Niebuhr's political realism; but *both* Robertson and Niebuhr lack imagination, since they are unable to envision a polity beyond something like "America at its best." For Christians, despairing means settling for too little. But if the church takes seriously the radical message it has been given, we might call its life together "democracy beyond democracy."

In the end, what are we to make of Stout and Hauerwas, who in all probability vote the same way, despise the legitimating "war on terror," and care deeply for their communities—whether it is concern over building a hospital in Community Park or the new Durham Bulls Athletic Park? Can these two Americans find common cause? Stout is not interested in extolling a system of government; he is interested in democracy as a mode of engagement. He has in mind the modest public spaces that hold the most promise for achieving real dialogue. But what about the nation-state? In speaking about "one's national community," Stout is clearly interested in American democracy *as* American. We might ask whether democratic piety is sufficient to curb the excesses to which it has historically been prone, particularly at the state level. It certainly is worth asking whether America is itself a democracy in anything but name, or rather serves simply to legitimate yielding control to the elite. Stout

---

3. Stout, *Democracy and Tradition*, 291.

would probably agree, but not because democracy has failed *us*; instead, Americans have failed democracy: we have failed to realize the radical politics that real democracy designates. In this regard, it is possible that Christians might yet find in the radical politics of the cross of Christ at least as much hope as Stout does within an erstwhile weakened (but still kicking) democratic tradition, even in America.

# SPEAKING

CHAPTER 4

*Metaphors We Die By*

Caring for the ill is a great moral task that brings into sharp relief our convictions about life and death. Not only does such care place the caregiver in unavoidable proximity to profound questions, but also the acts of care themselves reveal the nature of deeply held assumptions. Even the language that forms our descriptions of illness indicates some level of how we conceive of illness; our descriptions of illness also indicate how we understand the significance of life when it is in good health. In short, the words used for illness carry strong interpretive and evaluative power.

Perhaps no group is more aware of the power of such words than those who themselves are suffering from illness. Some are critical of the way that modern medicine has made extensive use of the military metaphor in describing illness, claiming that it is inadequate. According to this model, the patient and physicians are fighters, the body is a battleground, and the hospital is a military compound. William May describes the many ways that this metaphor is expressed:

> We see germs, viruses, bacteria, and cancers as invaders that break the territorial integrity of the body; they seize bridgeheads and, like an occupying army, threaten to spread, dominate, and destroy the whole. Like war, disease seems episodic; it "breaks out," it overtakes us.[1]

To the extent that the military metaphor might be shown to be inadequate and, as a consequence, unsuitable to determine the nature and quality of care that the ill receive, the question is raised of how to speak properly of illness. What is called for is a new way of speaking.

---

1. May, *Physician's Covenant*, 64.

But putting the matter this way is almost to miss the point. Changing the way we talk about illness can never simply be a matter of resolve or Protestant fervor. It is also not something that could be done or should be done from the high level that the discipline of medical ethics usually presupposes. Such a change cannot truly be possible (and I use "truly" advisedly) apart from the shared lives of actual communities that care for the sick in their midst and will require calling into question the deepest theological commitments of those groups. It is only on this level that the military metaphor of illness can be resisted.

In this chapter, I will advance the thesis that the linguistic philosophy of modernity has left us with such an impoverished account of the role of language—specifically metaphorical language—that it has been nearly impossible to plead the case of those whose suffering is made worse by descriptions of their illnesses that are foreign to their own experience. However, recent developments in the philosophy of language, which some are calling postmodern, have allowed for an articulation of metaphor such that the body and the community can be recovered as significant moral players. I will suggest that the church and not medicine must then become the locus for the defining practices that give rise to any account of suffering that hopes to be intelligible in light of the gospel of Jesus Christ. In other words, the greatest moral dilemma facing the church with regard to the sick is how to be a people who are able truthfully to narrate the lives and deaths of those in our midst. I hope to show that a discussion of illness and its metaphors bears significantly on this dilemma.

Specifically, I will argue that only a church committed to nonviolence is able to provide the kind of care necessary to speak about illness on behalf of those who are sick. Only such a church is able to reject the inadequate military metaphor of illness by giving an account of death that does not underwrite the pursuit of securing life at all costs. This community of faith is the only way of resisting a world made possible by military violence in which death can only justifiably be described in violent terms. The language of violence is necessary lest such a world become subject to the kind of scrutiny that would render death in military conquest unintelligible. As an alternative, a nonviolent church declares that this unintelligibility is, in fact, central to an account of illness and death that does not need to turn the sick into war heroes since it follows a crucified Lord.

This chapter will be divided into three parts: The first outlines various theories of metaphor including modern and postmodern views. The second examines Susan Sontag's rejection of the military metaphor for illness in light of these theories. I will show reasons why her rejection is not ultimately sustainable and cannot offer an alternative since it underwrites modernist assumptions that make the metaphor inevitable. In response to this examination, the third part attempts to set forth the alternative that nonviolent Christians can offer in care for the ill. I must beg the reader's patience through the first part where I must establish the linguistic framework at some length. I hope that it will become clear how this linguistic framework bears significantly on the conclusions I suggest regarding nonviolence and the care for the ill.

THEORIES OF METAPHOR

The reigning model of reasoning during the modern period involved the disembodied mind. Free from the particularities of time and place, the mind could arrive at universal truths equally free from such constraints. René Descartes typified this kind of rational epistemology, which set the stage for several hundred years of subsequent philosophy. The radical Cartesian dualism of mind and body was meant to save reasoning from the contingencies of human particularity. Similarly, the radically autonomous personhood of Immanuel Kant's philosophy attributed moral reasoning to the Cartesian concept of universality. This empowered individuals to make universal moral claims about what constitutes right and wrong actions.

This model of rationality has been radically called into question by recent philosophical movements that some are calling postmodern. One of the triumphs of these movements has been the realization and demonstration that the mind is embodied. Instead of being free from the body—or, at least, able to break free from the body—the mind *is* the body, which is to say that it finds itself constituted by the particular times, places, and experiences in which the body moves.

For the past twenty years, since the publication of their influential book, *Metaphors We Live By*, George Lakoff and Mark Johnson have attempted to show how findings in cognitive science can be used to critique the modern philosophy that is based on assumptions of the disembodied mind. They aim to show that the body's experience of the world plays out in continuity between the sensorimotor apparatus and the brain's rationality. As neural beings, humans categorize and form abstract concepts based on the embodiment of the mind, that is, through the body's movements in and interactions with the world.

A strong corollary to the embodied mind has emerged in the philosophy of language. Here, it has been common to assume that words have meaning apart from the contexts of their use. This move coincides with the assumption that the mind deals with concepts and ideas irrespective of its "context" which is the body itself. Postmodernity has given rise to a philosophy of language in which the meanings of words are embedded in their contexts.

Ludwig Wittgenstein argued against theories of language based solely on correspondence. He opened his *Philosophical Investigations* with a quotation from St. Augustine's *Confessions* in which Augustine describes the way he learned what things were called based on the utterances of his elders and their pointing at the corresponding objects. Over time he came to understand how these utterances were to be strung together into sentences and thereby to constitute a language. This way of understanding language as correspondence (that is, as correspondence to things in reality) became the object of Wittgenstein's critique.[2]

For Wittgenstein, language is inseparable from the context of its use. Those contexts are "forms of life" in which those who agree to speak in a certain way attribute meaning to their speech on account of shared behaviors and assumptions that accompany that speech when it is used in particular ways. Wittgenstein's account of language-in-use resembles the description that Lakoff and Johnson offer regarding the body's interaction with the world. The sensorimotor dimension that Lakoff and Johnson stress is operative along with the social dimensions. As Johnson remarks,

> We do not see the "social" as ultimately separable from other embodied aspects of meaning, conceptualization, and language. However, there we would never try to reduce social practices, values, and institutions in an eliminative fashion. The "social" and "cultural" are levels of meaning, action, and organization that have their own identity and motivating force.[3]

---

2. Wittgenstein, *Philosophical Investigations*, sec. 1.
3. Mark Johnson, personal correspondence, December 12, 2001.

The mind's embodiments as both a social and neural entity are not easily separable. The benefit of the analysis that Lakoff and Johnson offer is to show how the body's physical interaction with the world constitutes a kind of form of life. As a domain, this form of life is widely shared since physically interfacing with the world is fundamental to being. As such, the sensorimotor dimension is more basic to human experience than specific social and cultural forms and is often more determinative for the categorization of much abstract thought.

As Lakoff and Johnson observe, our language reflects the fact that abstract thought is largely metaphorically shaped. For example, it is common to speak about the abstract concept of time according to the metaphor "time is money." This explains locutions such as "You're *wasting* my time," "This gadget will *save* you hours," "How do you *spend* your time these days?" "Do you *have* much time *left*?" and "I *lost* a lot of time when I got sick."[4] Speaking about time in this way is speaking metaphorically, because no one claims to be asserting that time *really is* money in the strict ontological sense, and yet our actions and beliefs related to time reflect that we *really do* hold the concept of time in the same manner as we hold the concept of money. Since we act toward time just as we act toward money, we conceptualize one in terms of the other.[5]

In addition to the metaphorical concept "time is money," which is culture-specific and arises from the nature of social organization and interaction, the concept of time as spatially represented is more basic to human experience. This spatial metaphor takes the form of the past as behind ("that's behind us"), the present as "here," and the future as in front ("let's look ahead to the future"). Lakoff and Johnson suggest that this way of conceiving of time combines the everyday experiences of "motion-situations" with "time-defining events," which is to say that since bodies move within time, the concept of time is automatically mapped to the concept of movement.[6]

---

4. Lakoff and Johnson, *Metaphors We Live By*, 8.

5. These two sentences show that it is not a settled matter whether experience precedes concepts or the other way round. Lakoff and Johnson write, "When we do something we shouldn't have done and *bawl ourselves out*, many of us experience a sense of shame. And when we *betray ourselves*, we can experience a sense of guilt. Such phenomena raise a chicken-egg question: Does the metaphor fit a preexisting qualitative experience, or does the qualitative experience come from conceptualizing what we have done via that metaphor? The answer is not obvious." Lakoff and Johnson, *Philosophy in the Flesh*, 289.

6. Ibid., 151.

The "time is money" metaphor is typically operative along with the spatially conceived understanding of time and need not compete for conceptual dominance. It is common for people to function according to mutually informative or even contradictory metaphorical concepts.[7]

Rhetoricians have by no means settled on a single theory of metaphor. Therefore, in order to show how the analysis that Lakoff and Johnson make might be right, it is necessary to delineate the boundaries of some of the various theories.[8] The earliest and most enduring theory was put forth by Aristotle in the *Poetics* when he said that "A 'metaphorical term' involves the transferred use of a term that properly belongs to something else."[9] In the modern period, this view was made much more absolutist and was used to underwrite assumptions that philosophy and rhetoric should be modeled after science.[10] It became common to understand that, in metaphor, one thing is compared to or substituted for another as part of a rhetorical flourish that could very easily be done away with in favor of speaking more plainly. It should not be surprising that metaphor has not been given high regard apart from poetry and aesthetic disciplines since it, on this view, cannot help but be inexact. Given Wittgenstein's rendering of the Augustinian view of language as correspondence, metaphor must be taken as a lie (or at least as a circumlocution) and so, in its applications, unsuitable for straightforward communication and for use in disciplines that depend on precision of language, such as the sciences.

Not much was at stake when Shakespeare wrote:

> Then let not winter's ragged hand deface
> In thee thy summer ere thou be distilled.[11]

There are, however, important questions of why and how this metaphor works. The classical view of metaphor suggests that something about winter can be spoken of as having a ragged hand, and that whatever

---

7. George Lakoff observes that "It is normal for people to operate with multiple models in various domains." Lakoff, *Moral Politics*, 14.

8. A comprehensive survey of the various theories of metaphor is found in Soskice, *Metaphor and Religious Language*. My brief survey will trace some of the steps made in Soskice's excellent book.

9. Aristotle, *Poetics* 1457b; cited in Soskice, *Metaphor and Religious Language*, 4.

10. See Soskice's observations of Hobbes and Locke in ibid., 12.

11. *Sonnet 6*. Even though this is not a strict metaphor, it is a metaphorical figure of speech. By using it, I mean to call attention to the concept of metaphor rather than a particular syntactic construction.

it is could be substituted into the poem (according to Max Black's account of this view) "by sacrificing some of the charm, vivacity, or wit of the original, but with no loss of *cognitive* content."[12]

This classical view of metaphor, which was reworked in the modern period to underwrite linguistic assumptions about the disembodied mind, has come under critique. The most basic and significant form of this critique came from I. A. Richards and C. K. Ogden in 1930. They showed that metaphors work, not primarily on account of similarities that exist before the metaphor calls attention to them, but that metaphors work precisely by *creating* similarities in the mind where they may not have existed before. For them, the use of one reference to a group of things is related in a particular way in order to discover a similar relation in another group.[13] The concepts of winter and a ragged hand interact in the mind to produce a meaning "demanding simultaneous awareness of both subjects but not reducible to any comparison between the two."[14] The metaphor is less like a bridge and more like a lens or a filter, which itself defines a conceptual boundary by which another thing or concept is viewed.[15]

According to Richards, metaphor is not simply a rhetorical or poetic flourish that could just as easily be expressed in non-metaphorical terms. On the contrary, metaphor permeates all speech from the "rigid language of the settled sciences" to philosophy. "And this is the more true, the more severe and abstract the philosophy is. As it grows more abstract we think increasingly by means of metaphors that we profess *not* to be relying on."[16] Richards defined metaphor this way: "In the simplest formulation, when we use a metaphor we have two thoughts of different things active together and supported by a single word, or phrase, whose meaning is a resultant of their interaction."[17]

---

12. Black, *Models and Metaphors*, 46.
13. Ogden and Richards, *Meaning of Meaning*, 213.
14. Black, *Models and Metaphors*, 46.
15. With reference to Richards, Max Black is careful about using metaphors to describe metaphors: "I have no quarrel with the use of metaphors (if they are good ones) in talking about metaphor. But it may be as well to use several, lest we are misled by the adventitious charms of our favorites." Black, *Models and Metaphors*, 39.
16. Richards, *Philosophy of Rhetoric*, 92.
17. Ibid., 93.

It is important to note that, for Richards, metaphors work, not by virtue of the interactions of words but of thoughts. The connection between the referent and the word or words used to describe it is not a matter simply of naming it (whether simply or metaphorically as Augustine or Aristotle would have it) but a matter of the total physical, psychological, and social context. This is similar to the form of life that Wittgenstein discussed.[18] Shakespeare's metaphor of winter's hand works or fails to work depending on the possibilities that the psychological context associates winter with harshness, the physical context supports difficult activities such as shoveling snow and not just skiing, and so forth.

What Richards and Ogden provide is a conceptual mapping for the kind of work that Lakoff and Johnson go on to do. They show that, rightly understood, metaphor breaks down the assumption that language is separable from context and, ultimately, from cognition. If Lakoff and Johnson (and Ogden and Richards) are right about the interrelatedness of language and cognition, the metaphorical shape of rationality in general and of abstract thought in particular poses no small threat to the modern assumptions of foundationalist epistemology.

However, the metaphorical nature of our embodied rationality goes largely unnoticed because that embodiment is only rarely called into question. Part of the problem is that metaphorical systems can be so elaborate, and even self-authenticating, that they are taken for granted and so are resistant to exposure. One case where such exposure becomes possible, however, is when the body itself suffers.[19] In illness, the common experience of the embodied mind changes, often radically, because the presence of the body in the world cannot carry on as before.

---

18. Ogden and Richards essentially described a semantic triangle among thought, symbol (word or words), and referent, which is a simplistic version of Charles Pierce's semiotics. Wittgenstein's sympathies with Pierce may have given rise to his critique of Ogden and Richards. Ogden had translated Wittgenstein's *Tractatus* into English for Cambridge University with Frank P. Ramsey, a Cambridge student. Believing that his book with Richards, *The Meaning of Meaning*, answered some of the questions raised by the *Tractatus*, Ogden sent Wittgenstein a copy of it in 1923. In a letter to Bertrand Russell, Wittgenstein said of it, "Is it not a miserable book?! Philosophy is not as easy as that!" This is probably part grand overstatement (in characteristic Wittgensteinian fashion) and part response to the comparatively simplistic depiction of language. See Monk, *Ludwig Wittgenstein*, 214.

19. Stanley Hauerwas shows how illness presents a case where the body cannot be thought to have the rigid boundaries otherwise taken for granted. See *Sanctify Them in the Truth*, 84.

Given the correlation between actions and language and, more specifically, between the body and metaphor, when the body suffers, the metaphorical concepts that depend on a healthy body's interactions with the world no longer suffice. In the case of illness, those who suffer are the primary ones for whom the metaphors increasingly fail to account for the body's present experience in the world. The nature of illness almost always involves the reduction of voice and so invites injustice. Those most in need of fitting descriptions of suffering are the least able to make them.

## METAPHORS WE DIE BY

In light of the above analysis of metaphor, it should be clear that illness presents a remarkable case. Metaphorical concepts depend so much on the body's presence and participation in the spatial-temporal world that when its participation begins to fail in the many ways that constitute the suffering from illness, the ability to speak from one's own presence in the world is diminished.

At the same time, the embodiment of language is not fully described on the individual level but involves important social aspects. The linguistic community is the locus of the shared judgments and convictions that give content to the metaphors necessary for abstract thought and speech. This means that those whose bodies suffer are disadvantaged because they potentially fall victim to an injustice of voice, which is to say that they risk being overtaken by communal renderings of their suffering offered on behalf of their failing bodies.

The novelist Susan Sontag fears that ways of conceiving of illness in the West reflect the sometimes well-meaning but very often damaging overdescription of illness by those who themselves are not sick. Her thesis trades on the damage done by metaphors of the body and illness, especially as these metaphors stigmatize and so aggravate the suffering of those who are ill. In two separate works, *Illness as Metaphor* and *AIDS and Its Metaphors*, Sontag sets forth a plea to eliminate the factitious metaphors that are employed when speaking about illness.[20]

---

20. Sontag, *Illness as Metaphor and AIDS and Its Metaphors*. "Illness as Metaphor" was originally published in 1978 and "AIDS and its Metaphors" was originally published in 1989. Here references will be to the essays as they appear together in one volume.

Sontag employs Aristotle's notion of metaphor as substitution.[21] However, her view is more modern than Aristotelian. Aristotle had a relatively high view of metaphor, as having the tremendous ability to contain truth: "It is a great thing, indeed, to make proper use of the poetic forms ... But the greatest thing by far is to be a master of metaphor."[22] Sontag's view, on the other hand, reflects modernist assumptions of language, and the concomitant rhetoric that romanticized metaphor, making it suitable only for discourse separate from the sciences. It is perhaps ironic, given that Sontag herself was a novelist, that her concern over metaphor in illness suggests, not that the modern demotion of metaphor was unjustified, but just the opposite: that poets and artists, and not scientists, should make use of metaphor.

Sontag admits that not all metaphors are destructive and that some are worse than others. She is particularly interested in retiring the military metaphor associated with AIDS. This metaphor "overmobilizes, it overdescribes, and it powerfully contributes to the excommunicating and stigmatizing of the ill."[23] Illustrating the ways that this metaphor gets expressed, she goes on: "We are not being invaded. The body is not a battlefield. The ill are neither unavoidable casualties nor the enemy. We—medicine, society—are not authorized to fight back by any means whatever."[24]

According to Sontag, the military metaphor is unfortunately both pervasive and inaccurate. Its ubiquity is owing to the fact that AIDS is not well understood and so cannot be spoken of confidently in purely medical terms. The metaphorical language provides an explanatory grid with which to make sense of those aspects of the disease for which, by virtue of their remaining outside the grasp of medical knowledge, no straightforward way yet exists of addressing those aspects. She notes that cancer no longer must be described metaphorically, at least to the extent that it was in the past. Now the most pertinacious employers of the military metaphor once again have recourse to relative medical ignorance, this time with regard to AIDS.

21. Sontag, "AIDS and Its Metaphors," 93
22. *Poetics* 1459a.
23. Sontag, "AIDS and Its Metaphors," 182.
24. Ibid.

Written out of her own experience with cancer, Sontag's analysis is admirable in that she has exposed the strong connections between language, perception, and disposition by focusing on the experiences of those who find themselves described in alien language. She admits, "Of course, one cannot think without metaphors. But that does not mean there aren't some metaphors we might well abstain from or try to retire."[25] But can language be critiqued in the way that Sontag goes about it? Can we do more than simply describe language and the contexts of the body and its interactions that together give that language meaning? Can rival descriptions be evaluated?

In his treatment of metaphor, I. A. Richards offers a briefly stated but important way of thinking about how metaphors might fail. Of course, if the correspondence theory of language is false, then metaphors can never fail in an absolute sense, because they never succeed in an absolute sense. Nevertheless, Richards borrows the idea of transference from psychoanalysis to explain how metaphors can be used with less than optimum command.

For Richards, transference is simply "another name for metaphor."[26] It is the misappropriation of a sign (or "vehicle") to a referent (or "tenor") in which distortion results from the interanimation of the present thoughts.[27] Just as a victim of emotional abuse loses the ability, on account of transference, to trust in even those who are trustworthy, likewise metaphorical connections can be misinterpreted and improperly

---

25. Ibid., 93.
26. Richards, *Philosophy of Rhetoric*, 135.
27. Tom Thatcher has produced a fascinating study of apocalyptic literature, which often employs "empty metaphors" as a rhetorical device. A metaphor is empty when the referent is missing and must be supplied by the reader. Of the book of Revelation, Thatcher remarks, "Compelled to fill this void [the missing referent] or surrender the metaphor to meaninglessness, John's reader must create a stabilizing intertext. The empty apocalyptic metaphor invites the reader to textualize some aspect of history or of her own world or experience and make this information the referent that stabilizes the play of the psychological contexts. In the latter case the reader does not disregard the "content" of the text; rather, the reader *is* the content of many apocalyptic metaphors" (Thatcher, "Empty Metaphors," 554). Thatcher's thesis turns on the theory of metaphor put forth by Ogden and Richards and presents an interesting case by showing that a metaphor can still "work" even if it is missing a referent. That such metaphors exist as part of an intentional literary strategy demonstrates that meaning is not inherent in the referent; meaning and referent are separable to such an extent that the referent need not be present at all for there to be a meaning.

deployed. The vehicle becomes unsteady because it is removed from its original application and transferred to a new thought-context that may only partly warrant the resemblances that the metaphor calls forth. A strong command of metaphor, however, deploys tenor and vehicle freely, and they cooperate by inviting discernment and appropriate behavior.

Richards's comparison of transference with the deficient potential of language is extremely instructive once we turn to Sontag's critique of the metaphors of illness. Transference is another way of describing the claim that Sontag makes in saying that the language of illness often "overdescribes" the experiences of the ones who are sick. Such metaphors call forth resemblances that are foreign to those who are actually in a place to "see" them. Put more strongly, only a sick person has the moral authority to question the language of suffering. This is what makes Sontag's account so valuable.

William May's analysis of the various images (metaphors) of the healer is helpful in sorting out their relative merits and flaws. He points out that "Merely living by metaphors tends to exclude moral criticism rather than to invite it. An image often rationalizes a given pattern of activity rather than subjecting it to rational criticism."[28] He goes on:

> Metaphors can deceive: the physician can only win a few firefights against death, but the full-dress military metaphor holds out the prospect of winning the war. Images, moreover, carry a demiurgic power that compounds the difficulty. Metaphors are demiurgic in the sense that they do not simply describe the world, they partly create and re-create the world to conform to an image.[29]

Like May's, Sontag's appeal admits to the fact that not all metaphors are created equal, and some might just as well be replaced. Despite the strengths of her project, however, it ultimately fails on account of its reliance on an outmoded, modern theory of language and its concomitant understanding of metaphor.

Not only has the Aristotelian notion of metaphor as substitution been shown seriously to be flawed, but also metaphors are much more central to language than Sontag's analysis admits. As the previous section of this chapter has shown, metaphors require common assent for their use. This common use, in turn, bears on common embodiment for

---

28. May, *Physician's Covenant*, 20.
29. Ibid.

a metaphorical utterance to be successful. In other words, an individual experience could, in theory, give rise to a metaphorical utterance, but the individual experience would in no way guarantee that the utterance would be understood. Instead, it is the common experiences of those who would use metaphorical language that enables such understanding.

Putting the matter this way (that communal experience bears on the shared metaphor) accounts for the destructiveness of the military metaphor that Sontag wants so much to resist. She has observed that the military metaphor is now employed with regard to AIDS to the degree that it once was applied to cancer. Since science has been able to explain cancer much more adequately, the military metaphor has largely been dropped. Sontag's assumption is that once AIDS can be described more adequately by science, it too will cease eliciting the military metaphor. Not only does this assumption wrongly suppose the objectivity of "describing something scientifically," as Richards points out, but it also fails to account for the reasons that the metaphor came about in the first place.[30]

Metaphors not only arise out of the common experiences of members of a community; they also frame the ways that the community comprehends the cases described metaphorically. We shall now turn to the linguistic communities of sufferers and caregivers.

## WHO SPEAKS FOR THE BODY?

Why is the set of military metaphors so persistent? Sontag is right to insist that they must be discarded, but she cannot offer a viable alternative. Even while admitting that "[i]ts converse, the medical model of the public weal, is probably more dangerous and far-reaching in its consequences," she prefers it because it purports to be more "real" and, in a sense, less up for grabs.[31] She assumes that if only scientific knowledge could get us to a certain point where we could begin to be more precise in how we talk about illness, then we would not have to resort to the metaphors that distort the nature of illness.

This appeal is strong because it resonates with our desire to see the project of describing the world scientifically succeed. This desire corresponds to the presumption that scientific language is more basic and

---

30. No single work has done more to dethrone the supposed objectivity of science than Kuhn, *The Structure of Scientific Revolutions.*

31. Sontag, "AIDS and Its Metaphors," 182.

"real" than other kinds of language. It is less tinged with local variation and prejudice because it admits to no particularity. In other words, describing the world scientifically makes the world more livable. Sontag wants to "rectify the conception of [cancer], to de-mythicize it."[32] For her, this means replacing metaphorical language with scientific language.

This position, however, is not philosophically tenable. Richards says, "our pretense to do without metaphor is never more than a bluff waiting to be called."[33] The question is not primarily how to do away with a metaphor but, once a metaphor has proved inadequate, what made such a metaphor so powerful in the first place? In the case of illness, the problem is fundamentally not linguistic or scientific; it is theological.

The military metaphor is dominant, not simply because it fills a void that science cannot fill, but because in a world constituted by military violence, it is the only means left to account for the tragedy of deaths that we cannot control. Such metaphors capture our imaginations because we fear that without them, we would be left with unheroic sufferers whose untimely deaths are more tragic than we can bear. Any death that follows a battle with an enemy is heroic. By such metaphors, we distance ourselves from tragedy to the extent that we conceive of war as the only way to explain unexplainable death.

The military metaphor, therefore, is only the underside of the medical model since it seeks the same kind of explanation (eschewal of tragedy) that technical, scientific language does. This is most strikingly clear in the disjunction between care and cure in modern medicine. Sontag observes that we live "in an era in which medicine's central premise is that all diseases can be cured."[34] The medical profession has become obsessed with curing patients instead of caring for them, because it cannot but fear death. Unable to cure, medicine must concede that it has failed.

The reason that Sontag has observed a waning of the military metaphor to describe cancer has little directly to do with advancements in science's understanding of cancer. Although it is certainly true that more is known about the etiology of cancer, the fact that it is now more readily cured must certainly be responsible for unseating the military metaphor.[35]

32. Sontag, "Illness as Metaphor," 7.
33. Richards, *Philosophy of Rhetoric*, 92.
34. Sontag, "Illness as Metaphor," 5.
35. Of course, knowing more etiologically and being able to cure are closely linked. However, putting the matter as I have, I hope to show that a form of life which insists on

Being diagnosed with cancer is not the death sentence that it once was. If an illness has the chance of being curable, the healer need not give an account of that illness such that it sustains the hope that death not be tragic. This is the case, not because in such circumstances death is somehow not tragic, but because death is not certain.

Doctors are tempted to lie to patients when death is at stake, because modern medicine has no way of accounting for death.[36] It assumes that patients are not able to handle the truth about their own lives but, more revealingly, it assumes that medicine no longer has a role to play when a patient is dying.

Having put the matter this way, it should now be clear that the medical model of illness shares the same politics as the military metaphor. Both demand strong discontinuity with life in order to prevent the kinds of accusations that the reality of death cannot but bring against notions of good life that are incompatible with good death. Perhaps this is what Sontag suspected when she admitted that the medical model is not necessarily the better option.

If the overdescription of illness is a theological problem, a better option must involve a theological description of illness that has not made prior commitments to insulating life from death. A church committed to nonviolence then becomes a valuable locus of care for those who are ill, because it can give voice to those who suffer since it need not make war heroes out of the dying. The church of Jesus Christ is constituted by his good death (euthanasia), which was made good on account of its continuity with a good life, and so the church need not fear that death might become the ultimate trump card that would render life invalid. Joel Shuman, in his excellent book on ethics, medicine, and the church, remarks:

> The bodies in and through which we and those close to us suffer are of the same kind as the body assumed by Jesus, the body scourged and crucified. The pain—and the sense of isolation— that our bodies experience when we suffer has been experienced before in the body of Jesus. Through our baptism, moreover, God

---

curing also needs to insulate incurable cases from tragedy to protect the same convictions that prevent that a death might be a good one.

36. Sontag observes that "all this lying to and by cancer patients is a measure of how much harder it has become in advanced industrial societies to come to terms with death." "Illness as Metaphor," 8.

has acted to make all of us a part of that body, creating the possibility of really sharing one another's suffering. Just as Jesus' suffering was ultimately not to his benefit, but rather for the benefit of those to whom he was sent, so can our suffering and our sharing in the suffering of others in the body be seen as to the benefit of those with whom we share our lives—which is to say that the ways we are sick and the ways we behave toward those in our midst who are sick may be shaped by our understanding of Jesus and his suffering.[37]

I think it is worth pausing over Shuman's words because several key features of the analysis I have set forth are also found in them. We see that the church is the primary setting for understanding suffering and death, and that this understanding is closely tied to the worship of the church. Both these observations draw attention to the Christian alternatives to the dominant metaphorical schemes of illness and death.

The church exists as a linguistic community that is constituted by the routine practices of worshipping God, and so contradicts the prevailing language of the world, which is not so constituted. These practices constitute the forms of life, that is, the determinate contexts for Christian speech to become intelligible. By seeing the world, not according to Caesar and marketplace, not according to sword or phallus, but instead according to cross and empty tomb, according to loaf and chalice, the church rehearses resisting overdescription by a world that would demand an account of churchly politics that could only be given if the God of Abraham and Jesus did not exist. So speaking about illness in accordance with this rehearsal is merely another way of living true to the confession that Christ is Lord.

Perhaps the most important corollary to the function of the church in the world is the its constitution. The church's existence is more basic than the existence of its individual members. It exists as the body "from which we learn to understand our particular bodies."[38] This is why the Apostle Paul can write, "When one member suffers, all suffer together with it" (1 Cor 12:26). Shuman reminds us that in baptism we are made part of a body that gives context to the ways that we might discover our individual bodies, by narrating one another's suffering using the metaphor of Jesus's own suffering.

---

37. Shuman, *Body of Compassion*, 102–3.
38. Hauerwas, *Sanctify Them in the Truth*, 84.

This is why Christians are free to celebrate good death as an act of worship. We do not have to fear that our lives only maintain significance as long as death's significance is either ignored or overdetermined, ostensibly in the defense of life. If God raised Jesus Christ from the dead, then death is not the worst thing that can happen to Christians. It need not cast its shadow over life since by the resurrection God declared that life and death are both under divine lordship.

To say that the church should be the locus of care and that it can only be so on account of a commitment to nonviolence is another way to say that the church must take seriously its role in the deaths of its members. A church that cannot help its members die surely cannot help them live. May points out how modern notions of good death differ from medieval notions. "Most modern people equate a good death with a sudden death."[39] They want to die quickly, in their sleep or in an accident. A heart attack is preferable to cancer because it is over quickly and because we would rather not live dying. Therefore, heart attack does not pose the same metaphorical problem as cancer (and AIDS) because it does not need the same kind of linguistic treatment to be rendered morally acceptable.[40] The problem is more an issue of dying than of death itself. Dying is a state of life that we do not know how to live, because we lack the theological resources necessary to live as though there are worse things than to die.

Of course, putting the matter this way should make the assumption that "only a life without dying is worth living" appear foolish. This assumption appears foolish because all of life is but a prelude to death; it is one great dying process. May goes on to show that this was consonant with the medieval notion of good death as a slow death.[41] Medieval persons wanted to know that they were dying, in order to be able to prepare for it through prayer, reconciliation with friends and family, and the ministrations of the church. It was once common to die in the presence of loved ones, since dying and mourning were continuous events staged on the communal rather than on the individual level. Today most people die alone.

---

39. May, *Physician's Covenant*, 80.
40. See Sontag, "AIDS and its Metaphors," 126.
41. Here May follows Ariès, *Western Attitudes toward Death*.

A church committed to nonviolence is able to be the theologically legitimate locus of care for the dying because only such a church can offer an account of death that refuses to defend life at all costs, including with violence. That the military metaphor of illness justifies such violence correlates to an un-Christian anxiety over death's determinacy. As long as the church sanctions the use of military violence, it cannot simultaneously live as a truthful community of care for the dying, since it bears witness to a deeper conviction that life is ultimately about securing those goods, rights, and so forth so important as to be sometimes worth killing for. Such a conviction cannot help but see death as tragic except in the event that it comes while securing what is worth killing for, since at least that kind of death is heroic.

Christians must become those people who refuse to be described heroically. Shuman is right to see the church and not the individual as the decisive moral agent for resisting being overtaken by the legitimating descriptions of the world:

> It is imperative that the life, death, and resurrection of Jesus remain in some sense the norm to which the Christian conversation aspires. This requires the community to remain vigilant about the uncritical acceptance of the moral logic of the world.[42]

In response to the world's logic, the church offers the counterlogic of a death already experienced in our baptisms. In light of our baptisms, life need no longer be determined by the grab for more life, and death need not be considered tragic.

## CONCLUSION

Care for the ill is not simply an isolated activity of society or its individuals. Instead the nature and quality of that care reveal deep assumptions about both life and death, about what constitutes a life well lived, and about grounds for hope. That Western society appears increasingly to have no place for the elderly demonstrates societal avoidance of death. An aging body is a living symbol of death in our midst and a reminder that a life lived with no eye to death is an illusion. Therefore, we have no choice but to exclude the elderly from the operative social structures of everyday life. The same holds true for the place of those with develop-

---

42. Shuman, *Body of Compassion*, 112.

mental disabilities. Their flaws are reminders of our flaws and finitude, which means that they must not participate in our lives lest they challenge us to face the godlike strivings that otherwise go unquestioned and sanctioned by social convictions.

The Christian church is a community for those who suffer, because its Lord is a sufferer. This means that those of us who are not now suffering bear the burden of proof to show that nonsuffering is somehow normative to our discipleship. Along the way we are likely to find that those who are suffering occupy the moral high ground, since they are not compelled to secure the kind of control that nonsufferers take to be basic to existence. Just as the body's diminished capacities make diminished voice inevitable for the sufferer in a world of perfect bodies, the only hope for the suffering member of the body of Christ is a community that derives its moral identity, not from perfect individual bodies, but from the collective body that is Christ's wounded body.

This chapter has been an attempt to demonstrate that the military metaphor for illness is incompatible with Christian theology since it presupposes notions of death and suffering that are foreign to the Christian story, in which the life, death, and resurrection of Jesus Christ have recast these themes. Only a church committed to nonviolence is able to speak truthfully in care for the ill and the dying by refusing to make war heroes out of them.

The account of metaphor that modern linguistic philosophy offers does not allow for the kind of critique necessary either to make evaluative judgments (as opposed to mere descriptions of linguistic phenomena) or to make sense of the cognitive dimensions of language. So-called postmodern theories of language in general, and of metaphor in particular, suggest key opportunities for understanding the role of the church as a linguistic domain that can give rise to fresh (and yet old) models of death and dying—models that draw on the deep resources of the Christian narrative, and that ultimately will help to recapture notions of the body and the good life that are commensurate with being Christian.

CHAPTER 5

*Story and Eucharist*


The thought and practice of sixteenth-century Anabaptism seem peculiar to many moderns precisely because modernity has no conceptual framework capable of correctly understanding the movement. Recent philosophical trends within postmodernity, however, provide fresh models for reassessing Anabaptism in terms more attuned to Anabaptism's unique character. Some working within the Anglo-American strains of postmodernity have addressed and advanced post-Enlightenment thought in a remarkably successful manner, especially in regard to theology.[1] In this idiom, George Lindbeck is prominent among recent scholars using postmodern philosophy to help us imagine new ways of thinking about theology, particularly regarding the nature of religion, doctrine, and theological method. In this chapter, I will attempt to show the usefulness of Lindbeck's cultural-linguistic theory of religion[2]—in contrast to other modern options—by looking at the doctrines of the Eucharist and Christology in sixteenth-century Anabaptism. But in an age of so much methodological throat clearing, I do not just want to illustrate an approach. I will also argue that the Anabaptist tradition offers a valuable example of the form that discipleship must take if it is to be sustainable both practically and theologically in a postmodern era.

Lindbeck's theory helps to clarify three features of sixteenth-century Anabaptism, particularly as expressed among the Swiss Brethren: (1) an

---

1. By this, I do not mean to denigrate the Continental contribution, which, in some ways, is itself already theological and more naturally suited to appropriation for Christian thought. And even though a connection seems to exist between atheism and analytical thought, at least among leading figures like Russell and Ayer, its rationale is largely opaque to me. I at least refuse to think that such a connection is a necessary one.

2. Lindbeck, *Nature of Doctrine*.

interdependence of doctrine and ethics; (2) a penchant for occasional rather than formal theology; and (3) an emphasis on the church rather than on the individual as the locus for discipleship. To be sure, rarely in sixteenth-century Anabaptist literature is any one of these three points found independently of the other two, and I am aware that treating these three observations separately imposes some artificial distinctions. But just as ethicist James McClendon has described the various components of the Christian moral life by evoking the overlapping and interconnecting fibers of a rope, so I wish to respect the whole "rope" of Anabaptist thought and practices even while analyzing the various fibers for the purposes of clarity.[3]

## THE POSTLIBERAL LANDSCAPE

But first some remarks about language. The linguistic component of Lindbeck's theory, as detailed in *The Nature of Doctrine*, is clearly dependent on the thought of Ludwig Wittgenstein, who is sometimes called the first postmodern philosopher.[4] As I described in the previous chapter, Wittgenstein knew that when we speak, we do not just name things. When he opens his *Philosophical Investigations* by noting how St. Augustine, in *Confessions*, describes how he learned to speak, Wittgenstein does so in order to set up his critique of language as purely referential.

The problem is not that referentialism is false, but that it fails to account for the variety of functions that words serve. This is why he adds, "Augustine does not speak of there being any differences between kinds of words."[5] Some aspects of language surely do function in a referential way, but certainly not all—or even most—of them. By showing the various functions of words in even a very simple example, Wittgenstein demonstrated that a purely referential language is quite inconceivable.

> I send someone shopping. I give him a slip marked "five red apples." He takes the slip to the shopkeeper, who opens a drawer marked "apples"; then he looks up the word "red" in a table and finds a colour sample opposite it; then he says a series of cardi-

---

3. McClendon, *Systematic Theology*, 1:62–67.

4. This position is held by my teacher Nancey Murphy, who also places the end of the modern period in 1951, the year of Wittgenstein's death. All such dates are somewhat arbitrary, but this event strikes me as suitable, if only for providing a point of reference.

5. Wittgenstein, *Philosophical Investigations*, §1.

nal numbers—I assume that he knows them by heart—up to the word "five" and for each number he takes an apple of the same color as the sample out of the drawer.—It is in this and similar ways that one operates with words.[6]

Even in this primitive example, it is clear that the three words spoken communicate in three different ways. The word "five" has no *actual* meaning in this instance aside from the way it is *used*.[7] The word "red" only has meaning insofar as it is used with reference to the property of an object—apples in this case. The word "apples" is perhaps the only purely referential aspect in this instance, and even then its plural form is only as explainable as the use of the number five. In addition to the various meanings that individual words may have, *saying* "five red apples" can similarly function in various ways. It will only be interpreted as a request if it is spoken to a shopkeeper, and there are preexistent social conventions governing the ways shoppers speak to shopkeepers and what they hope will happen when they speak.

Wittgenstein goes on to show that the Augustinian picture of language is both inadequate and inaccurate. It is inadequate because it represents a limited view of what language is: "Augustine, we might say, does describe a system of communication; only not everything we call language is this system."[8] This was seen in the way that "five" is too complex simply to be a word corresponding to an object in reality (even to five objects, for that matter). Also, names of people are "names" in a different sense than are names of, for example, species. For this reason, pointing at a person and saying "Suzy" names something different from saying "woman" or "human."[9] Others, like Austin, enlarged on the many functions of language by observing that some words perform actions: "I do" actually creates a marriage where one did not exist before, given that certain conditions are met. (Saying "I do" in response to the question, "Do you ski?" has not only a different meaning but also a different—and in this case a nonperformative—function.)[10]

---

6. Ibid.

7. In Wittgenstein's words, "But what is the meaning of the word 'five'? No such thing was in question here, only how the word 'five' is used." Ibid.

8. Ibid., §3.

9. See Wittgenstein's treatment of the names of people in ibid., §40.

10. Austin, *How to Do Things with Words*.

But the Augustinian picture is also inaccurate when it comes to naming because it mistakenly assumes that the meaning of an object *is* the object itself. However, real language use is not like that. Words continue to have meaning even after the corresponding object ceases to exist. A person's name continues to have meaning even after that person dies, and, of course, it is possible to refer to objects that do not exist yet (if we are inventors) or that simply do not exist to us (if we are playing make-believe). Augustine's error was "to confound the meaning of a name with the *bearer* of the name."[11] In this way, the Augustinian picture is not only an inadequate model for the various uses of language, but it is also an inaccurate way of representing naming.

It is worth pausing over these first few sections of *Philosophical Investigations* because, as Robert Fogelin has observed, "Much though not all of the *Philosophical Investigations* can be viewed as an extended elaboration on these themes introduced at the very start of his reflections."[12] Wittgenstein is famous for insisting that language only takes on meaning when it is part of a "language game."[13] And like any game, language has rules. The rules of the language game are expressed as its grammar, which establishes the parameters of what can and cannot be expressed intelligibly in a language. These rules are set by a given community, which uses a language in a particular way, which is to say, in ways determined by that community's practices. It is crucial that rules are connected to practice since a proficiency in rule following is not separable from a proficiency in language use, meaning that one can *follow* the rules without having learned them explicitly but having only learned the language. This also means that rules may change over time, even in ways that go unnoticed until someone comments on practice (which is why dictionaries constantly need updating; grammars do too).

A language community, therefore, can never claim to have "set" its grammar once and for all; but likewise it can never genuinely claim to have no rules. A people with genuinely no rules could only be a people who quite literally do nothing. From the above example involving a shopkeeper and a customer, the word "five" takes on meaning only because people engage in the practice of counting things. Likewise the

11. Wittgenstein, *Philosophical Investigations*, §40.
12. Fogelin, "Wittgenstein's Critique of Philosophy," 57.
13. This phrase is introduced in Wittgenstein, *Philosophical Investigations*, §19.

Wittgensteinian example sentence "This room has length" has meaning simply because people measure things.[14] It is not always easy to know where to draw the distinction between what it is for an object to have a property, and the practices that give intelligibility to comments on that property.[15] But this only means that language is itself a practice that is bound up with all other practices insofar as we talk about them.

For Wittgenstein, the truth of a proposition has to do with how well it correlates with the forms of life it is meant to describe.[16] Truth claims are mediated within a language game by the grammar rules involved, so that the claims can be said to be true insofar as the rules are followed. So "This room has length" can be said to be true, not because the room has been measured and the statement thus verified as true, but simply because there exists such a thing as the practice of measurement. We know that rooms have length even before we measure them, because our linguistic practice does not permit talk of rooms with no spatiality. A whole language game then can be judged by how authentic it is, which is to say, how successful it is at sustaining a form of life. In this example, we would ask how successful our talking about rooms is to our inhabiting them, whether our referring to them is faithful to our entering and leaving them, and so on.

---

14. Zorn, "Grammar, Doctrines, and Practice," 510. Zorn's example is similar to Wittgenstein's "Every rod has length" in *Philosophical Investigations*, §251.

15. In this regard, we may think about the appropriately uncertain distinction that Alasdair MacIntyre makes between virtues and practices in MacIntyre, *Whose Justice? Which Rationality?* and in *After Virtue*. Practices are rule governed, but the engendering of virtue is not directly related to following rules even though for Aristotle, laws (which are rules at the level of a society) exist in order to make virtuous citizens (see *Nicomachean Ethics*, book 10). The uncertainty lies in the fact that there is more to the proficient practice of something than following rules: workers always bring more to their work than their job descriptions enumerate. It is important that virtue is more closely tied to proficient practice, as this makes clear that rules without practice (that is, grammar without people who speak a language) simply makes no sense. For MacIntyre, practices are not primarily about attaining virtues or making virtuous people. On this side of the Enlightenment and other rejections of Aristotle, it can appear this way: we are so considerably "after virtue" that as moral thinkers we can become obsessed with getting virtue back, and the way is through practices. But really, virtues are more a by-product of practices done for their own sakes. A fisherman needs to catch fish and so develops the skills necessary to do so well, and in the process becomes a better person, but not because he aimed at that. Perhaps the spirit of modernity can be characterized by wanting to become better people without actually recognizing the need to be good at anything.

16. Wittgenstein, *Philosophical Investigations*, §241.

These are trivial examples, of course. But linking truth with authenticity holds, since all truth claims are made linguistically and are, therefore, governed by rules of grammar, which, in turn, are governed by forms of life.[17] According to Wittgenstein, disagreements arise between people not over questions about the correct use of rules but over the practices to which rules are meant to relate, which is to say, over forms of life.[18]

Expanding on this link between truth and forms of life has appealed to theologians and ethicists. Perhaps Lindbeck took his cue from Wittgenstein's identification, albeit cryptic, of "Theology as grammar."[19] In any case, his indebtedness is clear, particularly in his assertion that religion is akin to language. Like language in general, religious language is devoid of propositional force to the extent that the corresponding actions of the user of that language fail to attest to its meaning or truthfulness. Consistency between language and practice is a crucial part of what Lindbeck calls "intrasystematic truth." In addition to intrasystematic truth, a religion can also express *categorical* and *ontological* truth. A religion is categorically true if it possesses categories (or a grammar) adequate to express what is taken to be religiously real. Categorical truth is a way of allowing for the truth of a religious utterance (a Wittgensteinian point), even in cases where such an utterance may not be guaranteed to be true or justified on other grounds. Hence perhaps categorical *adequacy* is a better term than *truth*. Ontological truth names the extent to which a religion conforms its participants "to the ultimate reality and goodness that lies at the heart of things."[20] Utterances cannot be true in this sense in and of themselves but are subject to confirmation by the ways that the actual practices of a religion give rise to lives that actually correspond to those things the religion takes to be most important.

Lindbeck's account of the varied senses of truth emphasizes that religious behavior does not inhabit a sphere separate from religious truth

---

17. "Truth as authenticity" is my way of encapsulating Wittgenstein's account of truth. I use the phrase with some reservation, because it might be mistaken to be underwriting the very kind of fitting-with-reality notion that he explicitly rejects. What is authentic is the successful deployment of the language game, not objects or propositions in themselves.

18. Ibid., §§240–41.

19. Ibid., §373. This is Wittgenstein's only reference to theology as such in *Philosophical Investigations*. For a treatment of this reference, see Kerr, *Theology after Wittgenstein*, ch. 7.

20. Lindbeck, *Nature of Doctrine*, 51.

claims; rather, it is bound up with those claims at every point. In other words, the ethics of a system is not simply the behavioral expression of abstract beliefs—as epistemological realists would have it. Rather, intrasystematic truth is a necessary but insufficient logical precondition to ontological truth.[21] Ethics, therefore, cannot be incidental to doctrine. Ethics and doctrine are interrelated in the same way as are behavior and language. Religious practices are indispensable precisely because they form the determinate settings that get expressed in first-order discourse and that are only secondarily expressed in technical, theological terms. Insofar as the second-order discourse corresponds to the first-order, discourse, a system is said to display intrasystematic truth.

## UNDERSTANDING ANABAPTIST CHRISTOLOGY AND ECCLESIOLOGY

These methodological observations help to locate the historical and doctrinal concern of this chapter. In particular, this notion of intrasystematic truth is extremely helpful for understanding the connection between the sixteenth-century Swiss Anabaptists' celebration of the Lord's Supper and their attendant conviction about the church as the body of Christ. Balthasar Hubmaier referred to the Supper as a practice "in which a Christian obligates himself to another."[22] For Hubmaier, as for all the Swiss Anabaptists, making a claim that linked the Eucharist to the body of Christ but that did not acknowledge important corresponding practices of fellowship and unity amid persecution would have amounted to falling into an identity crisis. Their particular ethic of fraternal love—exhibited in part by celebrating the Lord's Supper—is best understood in the context of the claim that to do otherwise than to love one another would undermine the integrity of what they considered an essential doctrine for life as the church. Indeed without the ethic of love, the theoretical question of the church's identity was moot.[23]

Modern models of religion, committed to systematic understandings of ecclesiology, characteristically distinguish between the church's ethical behaviors on the one hand and the doctrine of the church as the

---

21. Ibid., 64.

22. Pipkin and Yoder, *Balthasar Hubmaier*, 76.

23. The Pauline analogical distinction "the body of Christ" was originally set within the context of the *ethical* demands incumbent on disciples in Corinth (1 Cor 12:12–27).

body of Christ on the other. This distinction, coincident with the start of the modern period, reflects the emergence of ethics as a discipline separate from theology. To be sure, a disjunction between belief and behavior may be useful for polemics, but as Lindbeck notes, it then becomes unclear what distinguishes religion from other spheres.[24] Where there is an undue fascination with belief—that is, with the informational meaning of religious discourse—religion comes to resemble philosophy or science, a model Lindbeck calls *propositionalist* or *cognitivist*. On the other hand, nondiscursive, symbolic representations of existential orientations—what Lindbeck calls an *experiential-expressivist* model—make religion resemble aesthetic enterprises. While these two alternatives give rise to differing images, both maintain a strong division between belief and behavior.

Lindbeck maintains that these two modern options are inadequate theoretical descriptions of religion and doctrine. In a similar way, the modern bifurcation of doctrine and ethics also fails to do justice to the performative nature of Anabaptist doctrine. James McClendon praises the way that "Menno Simons, in his *Foundations of Christian Doctrine* . . . had so interwoven ethics and doctrine that the seam between the two cannot be found."[25] This interweaving is especially intelligible if religion resembles language. Ethics cannot be reduced to rule following, just as learning grammar can never make one a proficient speaker of a language, given that language logically precedes grammar (as religious practice precedes doctrine) in some respects. Therefore, a scheme that separates doctrine from ethics is as meaningless as rules of grammar that are never applied to the language they were intended to serve.

The correlation between Christology and the Lord's Supper in Swiss Anabaptism is a particularly revealing example of the usefulness of the cultural-linguistic theory's emphasis on the interdependence of language and practice or, in the more immediate idiom, of doctrine and ethics. Following Zwingli and Karlstadt, Swiss Anabaptism maintained a sharp distinction between the two natures of Christ, which proved useful when arguing against the real presence of Christ in the Eucharist.[26] Their argument is the following: In the incarnation, Christ took on both a human

---

24. Lindbeck, *Nature of Doctrine*, 16.
25. McClendon, *Ethics*, 44.
26. See Rempel, *Lord's Supper in Anabaptism*, 31–32.

and a divine nature. Following his ascension, however, Christ's human nature is in heaven and therefore unable to be present in the eucharistic elements. Therefore, the Lord's Supper is to be thought of spiritually rather than materially; that is, in terms of the mediation of the Holy Spirit rather than that of Christ's humanity. This understanding was not unique to Swiss Anabaptism but remained an enduring feature of all Reformed Christology.[27]

Of particular interest here is the nature of the conflict between the Swiss Anabaptists' christological predispositions (given their emergence from the Reformed tradition) and their accompanying ecclesiology—the realities of their life as the church. In actual practice, the common identity of Swiss Anabaptists was reinforced by a greater identification with Christ's humanity than with his divinity; it was verified by experiences more physical than spiritual. The unavoidable realities of persecution and martyrdom especially encouraged Swiss Anabaptists to regard the church in its external life as the incarnational extension of Jesus's life on earth. Therefore, baptism and the Lord's Supper both involved Christians' participation in declaring Christ's humanity by means of the same kind of revelation found in the incarnation.

In this way, the eucharistic doctrines of the sixteenth-century Swiss Anabaptists emerged out of the interaction between these two Christologies—the result drawing on beliefs about the nature of Christ, understood both spiritually (Reformed) and materially in the church. The Eucharistic doctrines strongly reflect belief in the spiritual presence of Christ; that is, in the participation of his divine nature made possible by the ascension. However, they also are ecclesiologically nuanced, reflecting the conviction that by virtue of his incarnation, Christ's human nature is present not in the bread and wine but in the gathered body of celebrants.[28] In his careful study of the Lord's Supper in Anabaptism, John

---

27. Still, for a compelling account of how the Reformed tradition has generally not followed Calvin's higher view of the sacrament, see Mathison, *Given for You*. Furthermore, the assumption that the ascension places Christ's humanity in heaven is not universally accepted. For a perspective that is extreme in its advocacy of the opposite, see Bulgakov, *Holy Grail and the Eucharist*. Bulgakov argues that Christ's humanity remains on earth and is thereby united with our own humanity "in spite of His Ascension" (ibid., 50). Bulgakov, like the Swiss Anabaptists, sees a eucharistic sharing in Christ's humanity and correlates it to human suffering for and with Christ. There is clearly more than one way to identify these things.

28. Writing in a very different context but, in my view, much closer to the mark,

Rempel observes that "where Christ is believed to be present in both his natures, there his humanity is at work in the external acts of the church, uniting them with his divinity, which is at work in the internal life of the church, in its collective faith."[29]

### STORY AND EUCHARIST AS THE NORMATIVE FORM

It is crucial to see that this interaction between two Christologies is an instance of what Wittgenstein saw in the interaction between language and practice. For the Anabaptists in question, the emphasis on Christ's divinity originated simply as a proposition carried over from Zwingli and Karlstadt, whereas the emphasis on his humanity derived from their experience as the church. The doctrine that emerged did not favor one option at the expense of the other but instead incorporated both in order to be true to the nature of life as an embodied whole (physical and spiritual). Lindbeck considers this kind of reciprocal causality between religion and experience to be normative.[30] There is a delicate interrelationship between doctrine and historical context, in which language plays a key role. As the meaning and grammar of language change over time, it can be difficult to discern the doctrine beneath it all. The theology expressed by that language may become incomprehensible because there is nothing more fundamental than the words.[31]

---

Edward Schillebeeckx defends the real presence of Christ in the Eucharist while attempting to correct excesses of neo-scholasticism that tended to focus inordinately on the change of substance in the bread and wine. See Schillebeeckx, *Eucharist*. Interestingly, Schillebeeckx shares many of the same concerns with the Swiss Brethren in wanting to recover the significance of the gathered church as the body of Christ. There are no doubt historical reasons that led the Anabaptists to reject Zwingli's spiritualizing and the perceived Catholic omission of the church—both were taken to be insufficiently concrete, lacking existential and historical poignancy. However, I certainly feel that if their ethos had not engendered sometimes-immoderate theological reflection (such as speaking about the church *rather than* the bread and wine), the Swiss Anabaptists might well have been more Catholic in their final resolution of the question of Christ's presence in the Eucharist.

29. Rempel, *Lord's Supper in Anabaptism*, 37.

30. Lindbeck, *Nature of Doctrine*, 33.

31. Schillebeeckx attempts to parse the language that the Council of Trent employed regarding the real presence of Christ in the Eucharist in order to separate their intention from what he takes to be the outmoded Aristotelian metaphysics of substance and accident that underlies it. See his *Eucharist*, esp. ch. 1. In this regard, employing the current philosophy of the day is parallel to incorporating from experience such as persecution.

We would be mistaken if we viewed this reciprocal interaction either as a corruption of pure doctrine by experience or as a limitation placed on experience by doctrine. If, for example, religious claims are thought to be solely propositional, then they are timeless in their original formulations, no matter how tied to ancient ways of speaking and to esoteric vocabularies. Ecumenical conversation becomes nearly unworkable since we will invariably speak differently, and so any "doctrinal reconciliation without capitulation is impossible,"[32] and the present case likely represents a failure to withstand cultural and experiential forces contrary to the purity of doctrine. On the other hand, if religious claims are thought to be solely expressive in character, then the forms of belief that *remained* in this version of Swiss Anabaptism become evidence of the believers' weakness. And from this perspective, it would be possible to dismiss the original doctrine entirely.

Lindbeck helps us to understand how human experience is "shaped, molded, and in a sense constituted by cultural and linguistic forms."[33] The cultural-linguistic model enables us to interpret the experiential influences on Swiss Anabaptist eucharistic doctrine according to the complex whole of religious life, which is to say, according to the involvement of complete people and communities in the forms of life commensurate with being religious.[34]

Specifically, for Lindbeck, becoming a Christian "involves learning the story of Israel and of Jesus well enough to interpret and experience

---

Nevertheless, I suspect Schillebeeckx is overly optimistic in his ability to translate from Aristotelianism to more recent phenomenological categories of thought. For example, I am convinced that those who are formed by liturgies that employ antique metaphysics are in significant ways also antique. Perhaps we often underestimate the linguistic formation that liturgy enacts, not least in Christian eucharistic practice. In this regard, present-day Mennonites must no doubt be greatly impoverished for their infrequent celebrations of the Lord's Supper and are thus generally far removed from their forebears, not only experientially in the obvious sense, but more significantly, in my view, liturgically.

32. Lindbeck, *Nature of Doctrine*, 17.

33. Ibid., 34.

34. It would be worth exploring connections with what John Howard Yoder calls the "hermeneutics of peoplehood." *Priestly Kingdom*, ch. 1. For Yoder, there exists something more basic than words, namely, the church. If today's church is the same as the church that produced the creeds, for example, then it matters that in interpreting the creeds, the people doing the interpreting persist through time. I am not sure whether Yoder would agree with this.

oneself and one's world in its terms."[35] This is precisely the testimony of the Swiss Anabaptists illustrated here. Rooted as it was in the story of Jesus, their Reformed doctrinal emphasis on Christ's divine nature afforded them the occasion to appeal *even more* to that story for the development of a self-identity based on Christ's *human* nature. They did this, in a sense, improvising on the basis of what they had inherited even while finally surpassing and being found at odds with their inherited, Reformed tradition in some significant respects. The Jesus story set the symbolic context for what would become the truthful, local expression of that story. They could not have been surprised when they experienced the suffering of Jesus in their own persecutions; neither did they need convincing that they were the body of Christ—a suffering, wounded, but ultimately victorious body, sustained and nourished in their fellowship of unity. Using the language of first- and second-order discourse, the Anabaptists treated second-order Reformed eucharistic formulations as flexible to the extent that they could better account for the first-order language of both their story and Jesus's story.[36]

The success of their efforts to achieve a theologically truthful and meaningful system depends on the capacity of that system to contribute to the practical achievement of its goals in real lives. It is hardly useful to consider the truth or falsity of Swiss Anabaptist eucharistic doctrine in a technical sense vis-à-vis its absolute correspondence to the real world. Rather, as Lindbeck would have it, first-order truth or falsity can be assessed "only in determinate settings."[37] Only in the particularities of actual people and congregations do religious claims take on propositional force, and even then only to the extent that the activities of those people

---

35. Lindbeck, *Nature of Doctrine*, 34.

36. In *The Lord's Supper in Anabaptism*, Rempel shows that Balthasar Hubmaier's language expressing eucharistic theology was an integration of Zwinglian sacramental language with what were taken to be certain ethical givens (52–57). Furthermore, of Hubmaier's work Rempel says, "Novel here is the use of classical Eucharistic language with reference to a communion which is not sacramental but ethical. This deliberate planting of old language in new ground underscores the radicality of Hubmaier's intentions. It cannot be accidental that Hubmaier uses the same concept, *Wesen* (essence), to describe the mode of Christ's absence and that of the church's presence in the Lord's Supper" (79). I am led to ask what it is about a sacramental practice that precludes it from also being ethical.

37. Lindbeck, *Nature of Doctrine*, 68.

and congregations bear witness to the truthful appropriation of those claims.[38]

Hence, it is not surprising that the writings of Anabaptist leaders and theologians demonstrate more agreement on moral and ethical issues than they do on points of technical theology. Furthermore, one often finds an interdependence of ethics and doctrine as well as a strong communitarian emphasis.[39] Consider the following from Conrad Grebel's well-known epistle to Thomas Müntzer (1524):

> Although it is simply bread, yet if faith and brotherly love precede it, it is to be received with joy, since, when it is used in the church, it is to show us that we are truly one bread and one body, and that we are and wish to be true brethren with one another, etc. But if one is found who will not live the brotherly life, he eats unto condemnation, since he eats it without discerning, like any other meal, and dishonors love, which is the inner bond. For also it does not call to his mind Christ's body and blood, the covenant of the cross, nor that he should be willing to live and suffer for the sake of Christ and the brethren, of the head and the members.[40]

Several things are worth noting here. First, as might be expected from the preceding discussion, Grebel offers no clear delineation between technical theology and moral imperatives. Whether present or absent, the ethics of "brotherly love" determine the theological significance of the Lord's Supper. The Supper of fellowship works, as it were, insofar as the celebrants bear witness to its truthfulness by being one with each other in the bond of love. Equally absent are both the Roman Catholic fascination with the Mass as a sacrament and the Protestant preoccupation with the nature of the Presence of Christ in the bread and wine. In

---

38. Lindbeck suggests that this same point may be made by employing J. L. Austin's notion of the performatory use of language: "a religious utterance, one might say, acquires the propositional truth of ontological correspondence only insofar as it is a performance, an act or deed, which helps create that correspondence." *Nature of Doctrine*, 65. Some would prefer a "stronger" account of truth, involving absolutist language, but this is precisely the kind of reasoning Lindbeck would have us discard, as it is an example of the residue left by modernity. Only modernity was able to convince us that abstract statements are "stronger" than concrete ones.

39. Franklin H. Littell takes communitarian ecclesiology to be foundational to understanding Anabaptism in his well-known book, *Anabaptist View of the Church*.

40. "Letters to Thomas Müntzer by Conrad Grebel and Friends," in Williams and Mergal, *Spiritual and Anabaptist Writers*, 76.

contrast to Catholic and Protestant attempts to provide theologies that were ostensibly true regardless of time and place, Grebel made explicit use of the contextual nature of Christian practice to suggest a theology sustainable only by the true appropriation of that theology. Put simply, his eucharistic doctrine was designed to be meaningful only when something was done about it.

A second point worth noting in Grebel's *Letter* is the way his ideas attest to the blending of the two christological emphases noted above. Following a Reformed Christology, the bread is "simply bread." Yet following a Christology conditioned by their experience as the church, with faith and brotherly love the church is both "one bread and one body." The church thereby extends the incarnational reality of Christ's humanity. This was Grebel's answer to the question of what happened to Jesus's body following the ascension, which removed his humanity from history. Rempel has shown that this same idea is also present in the Christologies of Balthasar Hubmaier and Pilgram Marpeck.[41]

This emphasis on the human nature of Christ helps to explain the sixteenth-century Swiss Anabaptist penchant for occasional rather than formal theology. It is appropriate that a church that believes itself to be the extension of the human, physical body of Christ should function as Christ did. It must act and respond according to the same historical specificity found in the stories of Jesus. Just as these stories refer to a real person in a particular time and place, so must the theological witness of the church. It is to the credit of sixteenth-century Anabaptism that the theology it produced is contextually rooted and occasionally determined in the forms of apologetic confessions and instructions to specific congregations, as in the case of Grebel's *Letter* to Müntzer, Sattler's letter to the congregation at Horb, or the many missives of Menno Simons. Such particular forms are necessary because they furnish the kinds of contexts necessary to provide theology the chance of proving to be truthful.

In addition to rejecting a sharp distinction between doctrine and ethics and accounting for a kind of occasional theology, this christological formulation leads to a third observation: it avoids the negative consequences of a spirit/matter dualism. Indeed, an overzealous emphasis on spirit, that is, on Christ's divinity, leads to an inward and individual communion. In contrast, emphasizing Christ's humanity as the sole outward

---

41. Rempel, *The Lord's Supper in Anabaptism*, 22–23.

mediating presence in the Lord's Supper can disproportionately exalt the church at the expense of the individual's faith. The Swiss Anabaptists rejected both these tendencies by recovering the unity of Christ in his two natures, thus allowing for the church's self-expression of unity in both its corporate and individual manifestations.

This holistic Christology is but an illustration of the kind of holism that Lindbeck claims must characterize doctrine if artificial dualisms are to be avoided, and if doctrine is freed to be true to the holistic nature of the human being as a "psychosomatic unity."[42] The individualistic potential of the Christology inherited from Zwingli and Karlstadt did not square with the Swiss Anabaptists' communitarian ecclesiology, which had been reinforced by their experience of suffering and unity.[43] Therefore, that Christology needed to be modified in order to be true to their experience in the way that their ecclesiology was. Anabaptists challenged a separation between Christ's spirit and body because it failed to correspond to the existential reality of being the church. They experienced unity in both spirit *and* body, in both ideological oneness *and* the bonds of brotherly love and common suffering. Thus the total gestalt of the community determined their theology.

## THE COMMUNITY OF THE STORY

The indispensability of the community is not an incidental factor unique to the history of Swiss Anabaptism. Rather it necessarily follows from what has been stated above about theology as second-order discourse; that is, as discourse that functions to describe religious practices and first-order discourse. This is the point Wittgenstein was making in his argument for the impossibility of a private language.[44] In order for language to be intelligible from one instance to another, there must be agreement

---

42. Lindbeck, *Nature of Doctrine*, 37.

43. I am, of course, using anachronistic terms. And I am not suggesting that Zwingli and Karlstadt were themselves individualists, especially in the way that we understand individualism in a modern, Western context. Rather, the exigencies of Anabaptist life demanded that the Christology they articulated make clear that the form of church they practiced followed directly from their statements about Christ. Their inherited christological statements tended toward a kind of expression that would so prioritize the interiority of the individual's experience of God's presence that, according to Anabaptists, an insufficiently communitarian ecclesiology was inevitable.

44. Wittgenstein, *Philosophical Investigations*, §243.

about the function of that language. In order for there to be agreement, more than one person must be using the language. In other words, common effects—which are partially derivative of and partially constitutive of the language—necessarily determine its consistent meaning. Therefore, the question of how religious language functions within the community, both to express and to determine its practices and conventions, is not incidental, but crucial, to understanding the language itself.

Lindbeck has followed Wittgenstein in asserting this point. For him, religion, like language, is "a communal phenomenon that shapes the subjectivities of individuals rather than being primarily a manifestation of those subjectivities."[45] Put differently, the language of faith flows from the culture of the community and opens up the possibility for religious experiences to the extent that it has been interiorized by individuals in that community. This is true not only of particular words but of all symbolic systems, including the myths and stories that constitute the shared interpretations of a given community's history and, therefore, its present identity and future destiny.

I find this to be an extremely helpful way to understand the implicit and often explicit communitarian emphasis in Anabaptism. Consider the following instruction given by Grebel to Müntzer: "The Supper is a sign of fellowship . . . therefore no one shall eat it alone, whether on a deathbed or otherwise . . . no one should take for himself alone the bread of those in unity, unless he is not one with himself—which no one is."[46] This direction follows nicely not only from what has been said regarding the nature of the eucharistic practice itself but also from what has been said regarding the nature of practices in general.

All practices, if they are to be given linguistic expression, must draw on significances furnished by a culture—which is to say they must be practiced communally. In turn, the specific form of a practice is contingent on the context of the community. This idea is built into the practice of the Lord's Supper in Swiss Anabaptism. Following Grebel, if the Supper is both a reminder that the celebrants are the body of Christ in fellowship with him in one Spirit as well as a visible commitment to fraternity, how can it be taken alone? A private practice of the Supper would imply that the individual believer possesses the faculties necessary to be

---

45. Lindbeck, *Nature of Doctrine*, 33.
46. "Letters to Thomas Müntzer by Conrad Grebel and Friends," 77.

in fellowship with himself, to secure his own sanctification directly from God. In other words, he would be his own church. In the same way that Wittgenstein has shown the incoherence of a private language, Grebel has illustrated the incoherence of a private "communion."

### CONCLUSION

It is hard ever to feel as though much is at stake in defending a method, particularly as grand theories tend to fail to deliver on their promises but typically deliver only under protest while they smooth over those contingent factors not easily subsumed. In this regard, I would want to qualify my gratitude for Lindbeck's theory. Applied to the thought and practice of sixteenth-century Swiss Anabaptism, it surely fares better at holding together doctrine and ethics and at accounting for occasional rather than formal theology—better than the modern theories fared, which traded in rigid bifurcations and meticulous structures. Lindbeck's theory also helps render intelligible an emphasis on the church rather than on the individual as the locus for discipleship. Still, as a theory, it has its limitations. I am not convinced, for example, that Christian theology ought to celebrate any theory of religion (and certainly not in an unqualified way) since, after all, surely many of the ways that today's church willingly accommodates its life to the dominant framework of culture owe to Christian belief and practice being too easily described as "religious." However, until we can do without theory to an even greater degree, Lindbeck's theory goes some way toward chastening our tendency to grasp at metalevel formulations by helping to locate belief more squarely in practice and linguistic performance. In this respect at least, I hope I have demonstrated one instance in which a shift away from the philosophical agenda of modernity might engender hope, even if part of our hope remains still to be fully satisfied.

In regard to our postmodern situation, philosopher Stephen Toulmin suggests that we must "welcome a prospect that offers new possibilities, but demands novel ideas and more adaptive institutions; and we may see this transition as a reason for hope."[47] Such a prospect will likely require and furnish fresh models of discipleship that enable the faithful to conceive of their participation in the Christian story not as adherents

---

47. Toulmin, *Cosmopolis*, 203.

to a creed or philosophy but as actors and actresses in divine drama.⁴⁸ This will undoubtedly involve a rediscovery of historical examples that can receive theological legitimization against the strictures of modernity. Such is the contribution of sixteenth-century Anabaptism.

---

48. I do not in the least mean by this to dismiss the importance of the creeds. Even affirming the creeds in truth is to enact a performance that is irreducible. For example, Nicholas Adams observes that confessing the creed in worship takes the form of a prayer (concluding with "Amen") and that prayerful knowledge is part plea and part confession. The ability to plead and confess is therefore surely part of the drama of faith. See Adams, "Reasoning in Tradition." At its best, the Christian tradition has always affirmed as much.

CHAPTER 6

# *Forester,* Bricoleur, *and Country Bumpkin*

## THE STATE OF THE CRISIS

The introduction of Aristotle into the Christian world posed serious critical challenges, especially at the University of Paris in the 1260s and 1270s, and much of what resulted from this introduction received formal condemnation by Stephen Tempier, the bishop of Paris, in 1277. Many thought that Aquinas had not sufficiently distanced himself from the heterodox interpreters of Aristotle in his appropriation of the philosopher for Christian doctrine. Today Aquinas's work is again at the center of a crisis, but in many ways an opposite one. Since Pope Leo XIII, in the 1879 encyclical *Aeterni Patris*, rekindled interest in Aquinas as the "master and prince" of Scholastic Doctors, Aquinas has been regarded largely as a philosopher who answers the instability of Cartesian skepticism:

> Students of philosophy, therefore, not a few, giving their minds lately to the task of setting philosophy on a surer footing, have done their utmost, and are doing their utmost, to restore to its place the glorious teaching of Thomas Aquinas, and to win for it again its former renown (par. 25).

In an interesting way, Aquinas was again cast as a key player in the right use of philosophy, only this time it was precisely his Aristotelianism that was celebrated since it was seen as the answer to modern philosophy's aimlessness. Recently Fergus Kerr described the "standard account" of Thomism of the past hundred years or so as being unduly preoccupied with epistemology, with needing to establish how something is known before we could say anything intelligible about what is known.[1] Aquinas was held up as one who had the answer to Descartes's epistemological problem but, as such, was made to underwrite the priority of epistemology and its very separation from ontology (and so theology).

The result was that Aquinas became primarily a philosopher with a "Christ-free theology and a theology-free philosophy."[2] This is notable in the *Cambridge Companion to Aquinas*, which is part of a series whose purpose is to "provide expository and critical surveys of the work of major philosophers" and so chooses Aquinas from decidedly philosophical ranks.[3] The editors of that volume are pleased that "philosophers who have no professional interest in religion" are increasingly reading Aquinas as a philosopher, and hope that the *Cambridge Companion* will hasten that interest.[4] In Aquinas, theology should be taken as making the same sort of connection with philosophy as other sciences have more recently done, namely, sciences like biology and geology, followed by physics and mathematics, again followed by physics, neurophysiology, and computer science.[5] But this identification of Aquinas primarily as a philosopher, typical of the "standard account," to use Kerr's term, has increasingly been challenged. The articles within the *Cambridge Companion* itself do not all bear up the intention of the editors but indicate something of its instability. For example, Mark Jordan, writing of the relationship of philosophy to theology in Aquinas, asserts that "theology is related to philosophy as whole to part."[6]

The standard account involves a separation of nature from grace that takes natural law to be autonomous from and external to revealed law. Eugene Rogers, in his study of Aquinas and Barth, argues that this kind of Thomism reads texts like the *Summa* selectively, and usually at the

1. Kerr, *After Aquinas*, 17.

2. Ibid., 28.

3. Kretzmann and Stump, introduction to *Cambridge Companion to Aquinas*. At the time of its publication, the other volumes in the same series of *Cambridge Companions* were all dedicated to philosophers rather than theologians: Aristotle, Bacon, Descartes, Early Greek Philosophy, Foucault, Freud, Habermas, Hegel, Hobbes, Hume, Husserl, Kant, Leibniz, Locke, Marx, Mill, Nietzsche, Plato, Sartre, Spinoza, and Wittgenstein. Since then, the scope of the series has been greatly expanded.

4. Kretzmann and Stump, "Introduction," 2.

5. Ibid., 7.

6. Jordan, "Theology and Philosophy," 248. I am grateful to Nick Adams for helping me see the significance of Jordan's essay.

expense of Aquinas's commentaries on Scripture.[7] Moreover, according to Rogers, within its readings of the *Summa Theologiae* (ST), the standard account fails to notice that even arguments that seem to stand alone as evidence of natural law's autonomy, such as the Five Ways showing proof of God's existence, in fact do not stand alone at all (that is, apart from the grace of *revelabilia*): Rogers claims that the whole argument in *ST*, I.1.1–10 "has a circular structure according to which article 1 demands something foreknown about the end . . . that article 10 supplies, and article 10 sets up a structure of scriptural authority upon which article 1 has already depended."[8] Nature is intrinsic to grace because all of creation is gratuitous, that is, a gracious gift; and knowledge of nature *qua* creation is also not outside the grace that upholds creation.

This is putting a finer point on Rogers's thesis than his subtle approach does. My purpose here is only to indicate how the standard account of Thomism has been destabilized in recent years. David Burrell, Victor Preller (Rogers's teacher), Alasdair MacIntyre, and Bruce Marshall are others who have contributed to articulating the instability of natural law in the standard account. For example, MacIntyre points out a modern tendency to prescind questions about goods from questions about ends in order to achieve a limited good (e.g., political justice), given either a Hobbesian disavowal of ultimate ends or where such standards hold no consensus.[9] This reflects an operative atheism that combines the Averroist insistence that ends be restricted to this present life with the necessity for political stability when it could no longer be assumed that the citizenry was Christian. In response, interpretations of Thomism repositioned ultimate ends in a nontheological conception of nature so that human good was discoverable in humanity *qua* humanity. Catholic moral theology is only now coming to terms with the inadequacy of this response. For many, it can no longer be taken for granted that, in an ethic of natural law as Aquinas understood it, we know what it means for something to be "natural."

This chapter examines some recent engagements with the ethics of Thomas Aquinas in light of the aptness of three suggestive images for explicating moral knowledge and action. As a starting point, we will con-

---

7. Rogers, *Thomas Aquinas and Karl Barth*.
8. Ibid., 55.
9. MacIntyre, *Three Rival Versions*, 140.

sider the way Aquinas described the beginning of practical rationality, namely, *synderesis*:

> Wherefore the first practical principles, bestowed on us by nature, do not belong to a special power, but to a special natural habit, which we call "synderesis." Whence "synderesis" is said to incite to good, and to murmur at evil, inasmuch as through first principles we proceed to discover, and judge of what we have discovered. It is therefore clear that "synderesis" is not a power, but a natural habit.[10]

Just what is a "natural habit"? It might seem that Aquinas would like to have it both ways, for what is natural is "known without any investigation on the part of reason, as from an immovable principle,"[11] and what is a habit, following Aristotle, is not readily known, since it is a disposition. But can some dispositions be natural? Aquinas notes that "habit implies a disposition in relation to a thing's nature, and to its operation or end, by reason of which disposition a thing is well or ill disposed thereto."[12] This means that a habit's ordering corresponds to the nature of a thing; but is the habit natural in the same sense as the nature of the thing is natural? We find two senses in which Aquinas will speak of something as being natural: specifically and individually.[13] Specific human nature is shared across the species (e.g., humans share the faculty of laughing), whereas individual nature varies from person to person (e.g., one person inclines to health, another to sickness). The specific nature is the way that the standard account has understood the sense in which natural law is natural. However, Aquinas is not suggesting that there are two kinds of nature but simply that "one thing can be natural to another in [these] two ways."[14] There is a place for habits (and so for the virtues) to work:

> Thus, then, if we speak of habit as a disposition of the subject in relation to form or nature, it may be natural in either of the foregoing ways. For there is a certain natural disposition demanded by the human species, so that no man can be without it. And this disposition is natural in respect of the specific nature. But since

---

10. Aquinas, *Summa Theologica*, I.79.12. Hereafter cited as *ST*.
11. *ST*, I.79.12.
12. *ST*, I–II.49.4.
13. This discussion is largely found in *ST*, I–II.51.1.
14. Ibid.

such a disposition has a certain latitude, it happens that different grades of this disposition are becoming to different men in respect of the individual nature.[15]

This means that some people are more possessed of natural virtue than others, and we might simply call this good fortune. Certainly good fortune must remain as a possibility for Aquinas; but there is another way to explain how habits may be natural, although this is not easily demonstrated according to the terms supplied by the standard account. I hope to show that the following discussion serves an explication of Aquinas's account of moral reasoning as arising from natural habits.

## THREE KNOWLEDGES: THREE IMAGES

Recent movements in theology, which some are calling postmodern—having acknowledged that the impartial moral agent is a fictitious construction, face certain challenges, such as the availability of and distinction between particulars and universals, the role of the intellect in discerning right moral action, and the function of the virtues. Three helpful images have emerged in recent discussions of Aquinas for delimiting boundaries in discussions of the moral life. How can habits be "natural"? How can nature be "habitual"? Traditional categories, particularly of nature, have prevented us from finding adequate answers to these questions. However, I hope to show that John Milbank and Catherine Pickstock's image of a knowing God as country bumpkin,[16] along with two separate pictures of the human moral agent (Jeffrey Stout's *bricoleur* and Charles Pinches's forester) can assist us in finding a way forward in this crisis.

### *Country Bumpkin*

We begin with an image not of humans but of God, although the kind of human knowing is made plain by contrast to this divine image. Milbank and Pickstock suggest that the first step toward recasting the human knowledge of particulars is to distinguish this knowledge from God's

---

15. Ibid.

16. I should make a procedural comment here. The reference that Milbank and Pickstock make to God as country bumpkin comes from Aquinas himself (*rusticus*): *De Veritate*, Q. 2 a. 5 resp. Nevertheless I hope that I am right to take this image as functioning paradigmatically for a larger thesis about divine and human knowledge. The reference appears in Milbank and Pickstock, *Truth in Aquinas*, 14.

knowledge. God has authentic knowledge of particulars since he *creates* particulars and is the source of their individuation. In this way, for Aquinas, God is like a country bumpkin (*rusticus*), whose knowledge of individual existences is unmediated by reflection on universals but rather is directly apprehended. He contrasts the ways that an astronomer and a country bumpkin know about eclipses differently. An astronomer has expert knowledge about eclipses in general but can only know a specific eclipse as a distinct phenomenon by fitting it with the general notion. However, a country bumpkin is more capable of grasping the individual existence of *this one eclipse*, since he has no expert knowledge to tell him that this is an eclipse because it is eclipse-like. Milbank and Pickstock summarize this point: the *rusticus* is "capable of a brutal direct unreflective intuition of cloddish earth, bleared and smeared with toil."[17]

God is like the country bumpkin; but the human mind is limited to grasping universals, as the astronomer does. Milbank and Pickstock go on to explain that, for Aquinas, human knowing involves striving after "bumpkinhood" in order to reach the kind of direct apprehension of particulars that God enjoys. Through imagination, the human intellect is able to approximate particular existences analogically through the senses.[18] But imagination is a reflexive activity; it involves the awareness of the image as the mediating principle for discerning all knowledge. So the intellect is not alone in grasping the individual significances of the sense objects. Because imagination is both analogical and reflexive, it cannot be limited to just the mind, but extends to the whole person—a complex unity of body and mind.

Against modern correspondence theories of truth, in which reality is directly apprehended and represented in the mind, Aquinas problematizes the idea of reality as such. Instead, what is truly real is so only by participation in the mind of God. Milbank notes that "there is no independently available 'real world' against which we must test our Christian convictions, because those convictions are the most final, and at the same time the most basic, *seeing* of what the world is."[19] Our truthful apprehension of a world of particulars is mediated not by the mirroring of reality in the mind but by an accurate rendering, through analogical connec-

---

17. Ibid., 14.
18. *ST*, I.51.1.
19. Milbank, *Word Made Strange*, 420.

tion between sense and intellect, of the individual participation in divine knowledge.

In this account we have an ontological "rather than" an epistemological approach to truth.[20] Not only is "truth convertible with being,"[21] but since all being is derived from God's Being, all truth (and, generally, knowledge) is rightly theological. This is part of the larger conviction driving the Radical Orthodoxy movement, namely, to show that theology trumps all philosophy by properly situating the content of philosophical categories theologically. More specifically, there is the challenge to modes of philosophical discourse that take for granted univocal being, that is, the assumption that what it means for one thing to *be* or to exist is necessarily the same for all things which *have being* or exist. For Aquinas, of course, the thought of how God exists is not directly (i.e., univocally) available when thinking about how anything else exists, since everything else exists because it is created; so creatures' created being relates to God's uncreated being only by means of analogy. Likewise, the way God knows is not univocally available as a concept from thinking about human knowledge, since human knowledge is related to divine knowledge analogously and is approached only through participation.

Milbank and Pickstock are certainly right to draw attention to the way that Aquinas would have repudiated later attempts to separate epistemology from ontology, even ostensibly in the interest of securing more philosophical ground for Christian theology against modern notions of truth. Furthermore, Milbank and Pickstock help us to understand that natural law is natural because of its rootedness in eternal law, that is, in God; and so knowledge of natural law is bound up with metaphysical claims about human creaturehood and participation in the eternal law of God. Brian Davies nicely describes the way this works for Aquinas:

> Does natural law derive from anything? Is there a law which is in any sense "above" it or superior to it? If we are thinking in terms of a code or list of precepts, Aquinas's answer is "No." But in one sense his answer is "Yes," because natural law, for him, falls under,

---

20. Milbank and Pickstock, *Truth in Aquinas*, 17, 22. It is not clear to me that one can have any account of truth that is not in some sense epistemological, else there would be nothing to be known by it. Milbank and Pickstock should more aptly be described as explaining an approach to truth that refuses to separate ontology from epistemological considerations.

21. Ibid., 7.

or is grounded on, what he calls "Eternal Law," which is nothing less than God himself.²²

It is questionable, however, whether Milbank and Pickstock have given us an interpretation of Aquinas that is able to account for the particular nature of the virtues and for the ways that their display is finally a matter of contingency. For example, Frederick Christian Bauerschmidt wonders if this kind of ontological account is not finally a case of the "philosophical tail wagging the theological dog."²³ In it the universalisms of modernity are not rendered unintelligible in light of the particularities, such as postmodernism has taught us to expect; rather, they are overwhelmed by a countervailing theological description that catches up those very universalisms in ontology and creation. Bauerschmidt notes that, in contrast, Aquinas himself simultaneously offered "a full-blown, theologically informed ontology, while at the same time paying scrupulous attention to the mysteries of the life of Christ."²⁴

Milbank and Pickstock have developed an account that rightly locates the seat of being and knowledge in God (in whom humans participate) but have not suggested how it is that the imagination is shaped by the virtues. If knowledge for the moral life supposedly turns on the role of the imagination, then the crucial fashioning of determinative images is accomplished by practicing the virtues, in particular the theological virtues. These virtues "are called Divine, not as though God were virtuous by reason of them, but because of them God makes us virtuous, and directs us to Himself."²⁵ Elsewhere, however, Milbank seems to indicate that the locus of decision and right perception is in the will:

> Moreover, intellection as more intense presence of God, already suggests that God must first be disclosed if he is to be desired, and thus that in us, as in God, *logos* must precede will (in God the Holy Spirit), while only a right-willing and desiring allows us to see what appears as a horizon of aspiration (though perhaps

---

22. Davies, *Thought of Thomas Aquinas*, 247. Compare this rendering with Germain G. Grisez: "Every participation is really distinct from that in which it participates—a principle evidently applicable in this case, for the eternal law *is* God while the law of nature is set in precepts." Grisez, "First Principle of Practical Reason," 376.

23. Bauerschmidt, "Word Made Speculative?" 429.

24. Ibid., 430.

25. *ST*, I–II.62.1.

Augustine realized better than Aquinas that we only ever see in the first place also by desire).[26]

Milbank and Pickstock draw our attention to how the universal of synderesis—a "natural habit"—is *natural*. But we also require an additional discussion of virtue to see how synderesis is, at the same time, a *habit* and how the Christian alternative is not simply another system.[27] In other words, Milbank and Pickstock just might be allowing a universal principle of being-as-such to eclipse the particularity of actual beings, thereby rejecting the universal ambitions of modern epistemology and reason, instead locating being in God, which is surely right, but at the expense of the virtues by which being is known.

### Bricoleur

Jeffrey Stout is clear that an account of the virtues sets Aquinas himself apart from interpreters who make him the would-be builder of a natural-law system. Stout proposes the image of the *bricoleur* for our conception of the moral life: an alternative to the "Esperantist," which refers to the failed project of developing a universal language arising from the traditions of no particular people, with the hopes of uniting tribes. The moral equivalent of Esperanto is a system like Kant's, free of the particularities of various traditions and oriented toward prevailing over the ambiguities and contingencies of those traditions.

But Stout is quick to distance himself from so-called communitarians, like Alasdair MacIntyre (even though *communitarian* is a term MacIntyre rebuffs), whom Stout thinks hold hegemonic notions of community and of tradition as loci of practical reasoning. Instead, "*Bricolage is meant to be a metaphor for what we all do when using ethical language self-consciously.*"[28] There is no moral reasoning in the unreflective application of decisions mastered by others and imparted by habit. In contrast, Aquinas made use of the moral resources at his disposal (particularly Augustinian and Aristotelian resources), incorporating them unsystematically in response to key questions: work that Stout terms *bricolage*.

---

26. Milbank, "Intensities," 465. The final words in parentheses were not included when this article was reprinted as the chapter "Truth and Vision" in *Truth in Aquinas*.

27. That it threatens to be just another system is a critique Stanley Hauerwas makes of Radical Orthodoxy in Hauerwas, *Wilderness Wanderings*, 197–98 n. 7.

28. Stout, *Ethics after Babel*, 337 (my emphasis).

Furthermore, Stout holds that Aquinas not only worked in a sort of ad hoc retrieval of pieces of various traditions, but that he even promoted it as a style of ethics through the practicing of the virtues:

> If Aquinas was not what we usually mean nowadays by a natural-law theorist, and was instead a virtue theorist insisting on the priority of prudence in practical reasoning, then he may have been not only a *bricoleur* but an advocate of something called *bricolage*.[29]

It may be hard to reconcile Stout's enthusiasm for *bricolage* as a mode and his claim that by it he "mainly intended to describe our common lot, not . . . indicate a preferable alternative."[30] Nevertheless, it is clear that Stout finds the self-confidently traditionless status of modern thought to be a resource for *bricoleurs* who would follow Aquinas in a similar kind of activity by way of his method and content, that is, his appropriation of various traditions and his placement of the virtues in all subsequent moral reasoning activity.

Setting aside for the moment the question of whether Aquinas himself should be described as a *bricoleur*, let us briefly consider whether his account of moral reasoning ought to be considered an example of *bricolage*. The standard account certainly makes Aquinas an Esperantist, a great builder of a natural-law system. Specifically on this account, moral reasoning is partitioned into two operations: synderesis and conscience.

In the standard account, synderesis and conscience function separately and consecutively in moral decision and action. Reason grasps universal principles (e.g., "Do good and avoid evil.") by way of synderesis, and then involves conscience in the application of universal principles to specific cases (e.g., "Does doing *x* constitute doing good and avoiding evil?"). This is summed up in the definition of practical reason in the *New Catholic Encyclopedia*:

> Human action is concerned with the particular and the contingent. But there are first principles in the practical order, as in the speculative, and a corresponding habit that enables man to come to knowledge of such principles, viz., synderesis. Right reason (*recta ratio*), starting with the principles furnished by synderesis and using the rules of reasoning (exactly as in the speculative or-

29. Ibid., 338.
30. Ibid., 336.

der), establishes conclusions that constitute the rules of morality. Conscience applies rules to particular situations, to what must be done by the individual here and now.[31]

This account positions Aquinas as having departed significantly from Aristotle. It suggests a division of will and desire from intellect that is foreign to Aquinas and that more closely corresponds to the modern tendency to separate knowledge from action or motivation.[32] The problem is not just that this summary represents too intellectualistic an account of practical reason (although it does) but that it presupposes that an intellectualistic account of moral reasoning can stand apart from the perception and appreciation of the goods of practical reason. The very Aristotelian notion of ends gives way to Cartesian epistemology. The attraction of this account lies in its ability to explain where sin lies, namely, in the fallen will that knows better (through synderesis) but lacks the desire or will adequate to act rightly. The Cartesian account is supposedly an improvement over the Socratic scheme, which is compelled to treat *akrasia* (weakness) as ignorance, a failure of the intellect.

But Aquinas did not Christianize Aristotle by inventing the will to function as the seat of deliberation for what the pure intellect grasps by unaided reason. The assumption that Aquinas did invent the will as the seat of deliberation in this way makes Aristotle's *phronesis* (*prudentia*) at once too contingent for a natural-law system and too determinative against the vagaries of the human will. Daniel Westberg, in his extraordinary study on prudence, suggests that this misinterpretation of Aquinas reflects the modern tendency toward voluntarism, giving the will complete decision-making power over the intellect.[33] In actuality, the synthesis Aquinas achieved remained closer to Aristotle than this: Aquinas maintained the full deliberative and operative senses of *phronesis* except that he moved the object of human happiness beyond this life. The crucial point to make is that such ends reside in God, and their knowledge depends on divine disclosure such that human seeking after them is bound up with Christian ways of knowing, which, though "natural," are not generally perceived apart from the kind of knowing made possible by

---

31. J. A. Ladrière, "Reasoning," *New Catholic Encyclopedia* 12:120, cited in Westberg, *Right Practical Reason*, 32.

32. Pinches, *Theology and Action*, 195.

33. Westberg, *Right Practical Reason*, 223–26.

the virtues. Aquinas does not doubt whether *phronesis* is the process of moral deliberation and action, even apart from the supernatural virtues, only whether they lead to right action, having deliberated on true or false ends.[34]

As it turns out, "deliberation" does not quite capture the force of what is involved in the moral reasoning that Aquinas has in mind. In the grip of principle-driven theories of moral reasoning, nature is self-evident, not the result of practical judgments that help one to discover the evidence that was natural all along. But goods are finally correlative to a nature that is by no means self-evident, and it is only by apprehension of these goods that the fullness of nature can be perceived as natural.

Clearly Aquinas was onto a project that resulted in an account of moral reasoning quite different from *bricolage*: he does not intend for the moral agent first to take stock of the problem and the moral and conceptual resources available for solving it.[35] Instead, the very way of perceiving the nature of the problem is bound up with the moral resources already deployed. Furthermore, we might ask whether Stout's image is able to account of the subtlety of everyday moral decision making that Aquinas had in mind. For Aquinas, the process of moral reasoning and action need not be self-conscious; in fact as he formulated it, it appears exactly to give an account of how nonreflective moral decisions get made. Having acquired the virtues, the agent's will does not repeatedly consult the intellect over moral principles, since those principles are largely not articulated or even acknowledged. This is apparent in Aquinas's discussion of the habit of chastity. The one who has this habit makes judgments by "a kind of connaturality" whereas others form right judgments through "inquiring with his reason."[36] Habits form a kind of second nature that is more like nature itself than like guiding ethical principles.

But was Aquinas's project itself an example of *bricolage?* In a new postscript to *Ethics after Babel*, Stout defends his earlier assertions: "A *bricoleur*, as I use the term, is someone with decisions to make about not only which ethical beliefs to accept but which ethical concepts to em-

---

34. In this discussion of anger and hatred, Aquinas notes (following Aristotle) that "hatred is more incurable than anger" precisely because hatred arises from the passions whereas anger is a habit and therefore less prone to transitoriness, *ST,* I–II.46.6.reply 3.

35. See Stout, *Ethics After Babel,* 77.

36. *ST,* II–II.45.2. See also MacIntyre, *Three Rival Versions,* 128–29.

ploy, and thus which candidates for ethical truth or falsity to entertain."[37] Given Aquinas's depiction of the unselfconscious mode of moral decision making, it would seem that if Aquinas was a *bricoleur*, then he was the exception rather than the rule.

### Forester

Aquinas intentionally structured the *Summa* in order to help readers to perceive the world rightly, but not by handing them general principles by which to interpret what they see. Instead he went about training them (an intention he admits to in the Prologue) to develop the virtues necessary to recognize the contingent nature of particulars without the distortion of having to fit them with universals. Perceiving the world rightly involves seeing the world as it really is. Prudence (*prudentia*), then, names the virtue of noting what constitutes a right and a wrong perception. Acting in a certain way derives from perceiving the world as ordered toward certain purposive ends and so disciplines the will and affections toward possibilities of desire commensurate with those ends. At the same time, training in the virtues occasioned by movement toward those ends forms right perception. This way of putting the matter reflects Aquinas's refusal to separate will from action or, as Charles Pinches points out, what is right from what is true.[38]

Pinches's image of the work of Aquinas as the work of a forester is specifically meant to improve Stout's image of the *bricoleur* and represents a reassertion of MacIntyre's interpretation, particularly of his extensive demonstration of the fusion of the Aristotelian and Augustinian traditions in his *Whose Justice? Which Rationality?*[39] I think there are good reasons for favoring Pinches's image (and MacIntyre's Aquinas) over Stout's, but I also hope to show that it helps us see the significance of the virtues not easily explained by Milbank and Pickstock's discussion of the country bumpkin. The forester is possessed of skills for the classification and individuation of trees so that she is able to see patterns and meanings where the nonforester might simply see an uninteresting grouping. It is crucial to the aptness of the image that the forester does not impose a foreign system but discovers what is truly there. One potential pitfall of

---

37. Stout, *Ethics after Babel*, 337.
38. Pinches, *Theology and Action*, 191.
39. Macintyre, *Whose Justice? Which Rationality?*

the forester image arises if seeing the world as it really is means merely being possessed of the right universals. But the forester neither imposes upon particulars a foreign system of universals nor brings together shards of traditions to suit a separate purpose. The purposive ends of forestry are bound up with the very practice of forestry itself while at the same time giving the practice its *telos*. Pinches notes that "we must see that Aquinas is about neither system building nor fixing particular problems by combining bits and pieces of traditions or thinkers. Rather Aquinas is fundamentally interested in discerning reality."[40]

Like the country bumpkin, the forester strives for knowledge of particulars in the pursuit of perceiving what is truly real, but it is through the shaping of practical rationality that this knowledge is (approximately) accomplished. Practical judgments about particulars are partially derivative of and partially constitutive of the principles of natural law. This means that the complex sets of concepts and applications involved in practical reasoning both depend on and approach the goods in question. Unlike the *bricoleur*, the forester is engaged in these processes largely unreflectively and unselfconsciously, discovering more and more the natural goods already presupposed in the activities of judgment and discernment (habits) that correlate to those very goods. In MacIntyre's words, "The precepts of the natural law are those precepts promulgated by God through reason without conformity to which human beings cannot achieve their common good."[41] I suspect that we begin to understand the importance of putting the matter this way when we notice that MacIntyre has given us a rather tricky definition, tricky for two reasons. First, it is paradoxical: natural law precepts depend on the *telos* of the common good, and the common good is achieved through right conformity to natural-law precepts. Second, it is backward: we only know what the natural law precepts are in view of the common good. In the first case, the apparent paradox is circumvented by the fact that the natural virtues are present to some degree initially, if only to the degree that they can then serve in the development of other virtues. Also, MacIntyre points out that a teacher is required, the authority of whom will have to be assumed at first.[42] Like the junior forester, the junior student of Christian moral training (we

---

40. Pinches, *Theology and Action*, 7.
41. MacIntyre, *Dependent Rational Animals*, 111.
42. MacIntyre, *Three Rival Versions*, 63.

might say the student of the *Summa*) subjects himself to a master, who names what is and what is not this or that (a cypress, a murder).

There is no simple movement from moral knowledge to deliberation to action, not only because deliberation need not be self-conscious, but, more important, because moral knowledge itself is not easily separated from the virtues that make possible deliberation leading to right action. This helps to explain the rather tentative distinction that Aquinas seems to make between principles and acts, synderesis and conscience:

> But since habit is a principle of act, sometimes the name conscience is given to the first natural habit—namely, "synderesis": thus Jerome calls "synderesis" conscience; Basil, the "natural power of judgment," and Damascene says that it is the "law of our intellect." For it is customary for causes and effects to be called after one another.[43]

The upshot here is not only that synderesis and conscience are "called after one another" but that their very operations are caught up one with the other. Synderesis is logically first, but it is not typically first self-consciously; instead, it is rather assumed in the kinds of applications made by conscience.

## A WAY FORWARD

Given developments of so-called postmodernity such as the disavowal of the neutral moral agent and a subsequent, general suspicion of moral universals, it would seem that Thomism, having positioned itself in opposition to (but tragically dependent on) these kinds of assumptions, is once again in crisis.

The Esperantist fallacy was to suppose not only that universality was possible; by way of achieving it, the particularities of the various traditions were taken to be contrary to practical reasoning itself. Even worse, attempts at universal, objective grounding cannot help but be self-canceling as they expose just how particularistic those groundings really are. Michael Walzer notes that moral Esperanto cannot help but resemble the universal claims made by a particular position, in the same way that as a language, Esperanto is actually closer to European languages than to any

---

43. *ST*, I.51.1.

others.[44] At its worst, Thomism became a means of detailing this kind of linguistic absolutism by way of natural-law theology and natural-law ethics. As a result, Thomism necessarily separated natural from eternal law, natural from supernatural virtue, and intellect from both will and virtue. Aquinas was made to play a philosophical role that he would have rejected. Nevertheless if Thomistic ethics (and Thomism in general) is again in crisis, then the above models represent a way forward.

If God is like a country bumpkin in his way of knowing particulars out of divine simplicity, then we are reminded that knowledge of particulars comes from participation in the mind of God. This participation, we find out, is participation in eternal law, from which natural law is derived, and so natural law cannot constitute a separate, sufficient system of moral knowledge. On its own, however, the country-bumpkin image would seem to rely too much on the will as the locus for decision, reflecting both an interiority and a voluntarism foreign to Aquinas. The image of *bricoleur* reminds us that system building was far from the kind of work that Aquinas was about. But Aquinas's ethics—which may well have been the work of a *bricoleur*—cannot be described as advocating *bricolage*, since moral reasoning for Aquinas may operate in an unreflective, discursive manner just to the extent that the virtues have been sufficiently acquired; and right perception demands no more attention of activity than right action. The image of the forester further reminds us that the virtues both aid in right perception (and hence right knowledge) and depend on right perception for right action. The apparent paradox derives from the fact that the virtues are in fact inseparable from all aspects of practical reasoning, from knowledge to act; and they are dependent on one another, meaning that they are not acquired all at once. Just as the practice of forestry involves the interaction of a complex set of theoretical knowledge with practical skills, so moral reasoning for Aquinas relies upon a similarly complex interrelationship of synderesis, conscience, and virtue.

By attending to the questions raised and answered (adequately or not) by these three images, I hope to have indicated in some measure how Aquinas might have thought about natural habits and knowledge as contingent matters of human flourishing.[45]

44. Walzer, *Thick and Thin*, 9.

45. I would like to thank Stanley Hauerwas and Denys Turner for helpful comments on an earlier draft of this chapter.

CHAPTER 7

## *This Is My Brother's World*

I am aware that my reading of Aquinas in the previous chapter makes him an ally of Karl Barth. If nature's participation in God bears on our natural moral knowledge, then nature's participation in God surely also applies to what we more straightforwardly think of as "natural," namely, the natural world, which is the focus of this chapter. However, in what follows, it will become evident that I am not attempting to draw careful distinctions between concepts like "earth" and "world." If by "world" we are led to think about the realm of unbelief, of that part of creation—exclusively *human* creation—in rebellion against God, of everything that opposes itself to God's kingdom and that the church endeavors not to be, then at least for the purposes of thought experiment, I resist making use of obvious distinctions between this and the natural world. This may seem quite bizarre, if not downright irresponsible. After all, we manifestly cannot have Christians fleeing the earth when they are called out of the world.[1] And we somehow suspect that while the world is and will be the object of God's judgment, the natural world will not. Some of this concern ought to be affirmed (particularly the former); but I worry that it can also obscure what the Russian Orthodox theologian Sergius Bulgakov calls a "Christian naturalism" that emerges from the ways that the incarnation exorcised the earth itself so that now Scripture witnesses to and against "the spiritual hosts of wickedness in the heavenly places" (Eph 6:12) and "the prince of the power of the air" (Eph 2:2).[2] Confined now to the "heavenly places" and the "air," these hosts and princes have yielded up their possession of the earth since the earth, and not just humanity, is included in God's redeeming work.

1. Jesus prays against this kind of flight from the world in John 17:15.
2. See Bulgakov, *Holy Grail and the Eucharist*, 58.

Is the passing away of the earth (e.g., in Matt 5:18) only to be thought of as a future event with no hint of judgment, an eventuality bereft of all moral resonance? Is God just "saving souls" that walk a neutral and passive planet? Bulgakov is right to suggest that, as common as this thought is in the West (and in some respects it comes more easily in modernity), it nevertheless reflects a version of ancient Manichaeanism. Consider, for example, in an admittedly enigmatic passage, that Paul seems more willing than we usually are to relate the world to the earth:

> For the creation waits with eager longing for the revealing of the sons of God; for the creation was subjected to futility, not of its own will but by the will of him who subjected it in hope; because the creation itself will be set free from its bondage to decay and obtain the glorious liberty of the children of God. We know that the whole creation has been groaning in travail together until now; and not only the creation, but we ourselves, who have the first fruits of the Spirit, groan inwardly as we wait for adoption as sons, the redemption of our bodies. (Rom 8:19–23)

Part of the problem is surely that it is difficult for us to imagine nonhuman creation morally. It is hard to imagine what Paul could mean by creation's groaning—the stuff of zoology, perhaps: its waste, brutality, and feral condition; the stuff of geology: its anarchic physical destruction—but he clearly pairs creation's deliverance with that of humanity: "we ourselves," the children of God. The redemption of the world through God's salvation, enacted in the church on its way to the kingdom, does not exclude the natural world at all, but explicitly enlists the same hope on behalf of both human and nonhuman creation.

Sometimes parallel claims are made to support a so-called "earth consciousness" among Christians. In spite of our tendency toward Manichaeanism, no modern, thinking person seems to want to be Cartesian. At least openly it seems that most academics no longer want to underwrite a sharp distinction between the mind (or soul) and the body. In the contemporary Christian idiom, this means care for bodies as well as souls, concern for the earth as well as heaven. Nevertheless such claims may be parallel, but they are not identical, insofar as they can still tend to disguise the ways that what is "natural" not only ought to be an object of protection, but ought to be given a prior theological narration that includes the story of nature within God's creative and saving work. As Martin Luther observed, "Sun, moon, heaven, earth, Peter, Paul, I, you, etc., are all words of God, or perhaps rather syllables or letters in context of the whole creation."[3] They are syllables within the creative speech of God, the word that created everything that is; and they become, for us, words spoken in the task we have been given to narrate all things as God's. In particular, nature calls out to be rendered by the more accurate vocabulary of creation, and in a christological key. The Bible knows nothing of this distinction between nature and creation; nature is always creation. I suspect that only by rendering nature as creation can Christians truly recover a sense that *all creation* participates in God's redemption, that salvation is cosmic, and that, until there is a new heaven and a new earth, every corner of creation hopes for it.

## OUR FATHER'S WORLD

The world is God's, not ours. This is, of course, a profoundly theological statement. The first words of the Bible tell us that God created the heavens and the earth. Not only was movement from nothing (quite literally *no thing*) to something accomplished by God, but we cannot even conceive of *nothing* since we ourselves belong to the *something* God created. So our very confession of God is a confession that he is Creator. Even more, it is an act of praise. All creation exists in gratitude to God, giving him glory through its existence and especially through the joy of being found within God's good care. Creation's goodness is bound up with its very existence, a fact that we are free to deny; but when, as praising creatures, we do not deny it, our praising not only becomes an acknowledgement of creation's goodness, but is the giving-back of part of creation—our voices and bodies—to God in a faith that *depends* on God's continuous goodness to us. By trusting that God will not reject us, we are not only saying that we are his, but also that the continued existence of ourselves and the world is God's nonrejection, which is but another way of saying God's grace. With this, we confess that the world does not belong to blind fate, that the changes in our world are not best understood as the results of random chance or the constantly surging forces of nature and chaos. This is what I mean by drawing at least a verbal distinction between "nature" and "creation." As I argued in the last chapter, what is natural cannot be understood apart from grace, just as our ability to know something on the basis of "nature" will involve participating in God's goodness, which

---

3. Cited in Jenson, *Systematic Theology*, 2:159.

is another way of saying that Christians participate in the worship of God as Creator of both nature and grace.[4]

Natural theology is still a form of revelation.[5] This is not first to say something about the status of knowledge God has made possible to everyone, but to say something especially about the account of creation that Christians are enabled to inhabit through the worship of God as the one who creates.[6] For example, in his discussion of Basil of Caesarea, Robert Wilken observes that Moses did not write about what could be seen, namely creation, until after he had spent a long time learning how to see things as they are. "For the early Christians," says Wilken, "the knowledge of the world began with the knowledge of God, and God could be known only in faith."[7]

By worshipping God as Creator, Christians learn how to see and name things rightly. We are given a conceptual framework and vocabulary to conceive of and speak about the world as God's. We give ourselves to the conviction that we do not lay claim to anything "under" heaven; we are not owners of our possessions, for instance, but their stewards. Consider a scriptural example. The prosperity of the wicked is itself a great wickedness as they steal from God. Still, a common theme in the Psalms is the objection to this reasoning on account of the fact that, despite everything else, the wicked *do* actually seem to prosper. For example, Psalm 73 registers a complaint against God's justice so long as those who are evil continue to enjoy their comfort.

> For I was envious of the arrogant,
> when I saw the prosperity of the wicked. . . .

---

4. As Stanley Hauerwas observes, "We are 'natural' to the extent that God has created us capable of receiving his grace." Hauerwas, *Peaceable Kingdom*, 160 n. 12.

5. Paul indicates as much even in his frequently misunderstood claim that attributes of God are clearly perceived in creation (Rom 1:20); after all, the previous verse reads "what can be known about God is plain to them, *because God has shown it to them*" (Rom 1:19, emphasis added). Aquinas affirms this in *ST*, I.1.1–3.

6. Paul is explicitly arguing that though God's attributes are visible in creation, these are not as an empirical fact being seen; God is not honored or given thanks; the wicked are given over to the objects both of their desire and of their abridged vision, which thus are made into objects of worship, that is to say, idols.

7. Wilken, *Spirit of Early Christian Thought*, 161. Also, quoting Basil, "Anyone who does not . . . enjoy fellowship and intimacy with God is unable to see the works of God" (ibid., 140).

> They are not in trouble as other men are;
>
> they are not stricken like other men. . . .
>
> Their eyes swell out with fatness,
>
> their hearts overflow with follies. . . .
>
> They set their mouths against the heavens,
>
> and their tongue struts through the earth.
>
> Therefore the people turn and praise them;
>
> and find no fault in them.
>
> And they say, "How can God know?
>
> Is there knowledge in the Most High?"
>
> Behold, these are the wicked;
>
> always at ease, they increase in riches.
>
> All in vain have I kept my heart clean
>
> and washed my hands in innocence. (selections from vv. 3 to 13)

Why do the wicked prosper, the psalmist asks, when *I* have worked so hard to live a pure and honest life? Even so, the psalmist recognizes that his complaint actually makes a verbal error, that it wrongly names things, that it is an inaccurate (for being an unfaithful) description of reality. The situation in which the wicked appear to prosper is not easily rendered in words without distortion so long as the psalmist describes it in the first words he reaches for. Indeed, "If I had said, 'I will speak thus,' I would have been untrue to the generation of thy children" (v. 15).

We share in the psalmist's objection when we ask whether God will ever make good on his promises to bless us, when we wonder why we do not have what other people have, especially when God has promised it to us and not to them. What, then, for the psalmist, is the answer? The psalmist's problem was not eventually solved by figuring it all out, by thinking hard enough, or even by receiving the right answer in any straightforward way. Instead, he discovered that he had been asking the wrong questions. Rather than discovering *why* the wicked prosper, he discovered that, in fact, the wicked *will not* prosper. He had been asking why the wicked are not in trouble and had discovered that, in fact, they most certainly are in trouble. This whole realization comes about as the psalmist begins to see the world as God does.

> But when I thought how to understand this,
>
> it seemed to me a wearisome task,
>
> until I went into the sanctuary of God;
>
> then I perceived their end. (vv. 16–17)

The sanctuary of God is the domain where the contradictions begin to resolve. But what is it about the sanctuary of God that does this? In the sanctuary, everything is ordered around the worship of God. Therefore, entering the sanctuary potentially orients us toward worshipping God; and as we worship him as Lord, we begin to be able to see and name things that are not oriented around the worship of God but instead around the worship of idols. The sanctuary provides the right symbols, stories, and metaphors for seeing the world rightly. If we use concepts rooted in acquisition and assertion, we will see the world as the world does. But the hope of having our perceptions redeemed reorients us around the terms of dispossession and sacrifice, of trust and gift giving. No longer may the world be described in the "natural" terms (which we may now call corrupt, despite how incontrovertible they may seem at times) of sword and shield, of stars and stripes, of dollar sign and pay stub. God's symbols are the equipment of sanctuaries: altar and pulpit, sheep and shepherd, bread and wine. The worship of God as creator, therefore, yields the Creator's vision, even if only, as Paul says, "darkly" (1 Cor 3:12).

Nevertheless, all of this can be misleading insofar as it can imply that the worship of God is a resource for the more serious activity of perceiving the natural world. It can suggest that our worship and our perception are two things, where the first aids and augments the second. Against this we must assert that worship not only *provides* a framework for something else, but it is itself a practice of perception. The world can never fully be understood as the contestation of violent forces—formed in fire and destined for destruction, red in tooth and claw, true as these descriptions may otherwise be. If nature is fundamentally agonistic, it cannot be good; it will only be enshrined by us in its alienation from God, abandoned to our bifurcating logic, and estranged from the hope that we are assured accompanies all creation despite appearances. This does not mean that creation does not groan; it only means that creation's groaning is, like our own, not a first principle that underwrites an agonistic existence, but an indication that God has not abandoned it. The ability to recognize this difference owes to convictions that are not only the *outcome* of worship but partially constitutive of what it means to worship God as Creator.

These are, as I have already intimated, Barthian theses and connect with God's creative freedom. For example, Barth comments that "creation is grace," by which he means that God did not need to create anything, being within himself every fullness and richness.[8] We seriously err when we speculate about why God created the world and give ourselves to answers that imply any lack on God's part, any loneliness, any deficiency, as though his being is eternally fragmented, split between contradictory yearnings, divided among incomplete existences. Against this, Christian thought has not needed to make recourse to Hellenistic doctrines of divine impassibility. On these accounts, suffering entails change, and therefore the god erected in response is a stoic deity, preserved in perfection but impossibly distant from creation and, theologically, a disaster if orthodox claims are to be made about God-with-us in Christ. Instead, Thomas Aquinas differentiated the kind of being God is from everything else, such that God is the only one whose essence is to exist.[9] Only God exists out of *necessity* (that is, out of logical necessity in the sense that one thing is entailed in another); in this case even though we may be able to speak about God's essence and existence as separate things, we are only making a verbal distinction conditioned by our linguistic habits for talking about everything else. But this distinction is not a real one when it comes to God. God's existence does not owe to anything outside God.

Putting the matter this way certainly clarifies what it means for us (and everything else save God) to be creatures of God. To be creatures is to be created, which means to be distinct from God. But being distinct from God is not the same thing as being separate from God. The claim that creation is a continual upholding of the distinction of God from not-God entails that even creation is not *outside of* God. So just as God's existence does not owe to anything outside God, neither does the existence of anything else, even though "everything else" is *distinct* from

---

8. Barth, *Dogmatics in Outline*, 54.

9. See *ST*, I.3.3–4. Part of Thomas's argument goes as follows: "Now it is impossible for a thing's existence to be caused by its essential constituent principles, for nothing can be the sufficient cause of its own existence, if its existence is caused. Therefore that thing, whose existence differs from its essence, must have its existence caused by another. But this cannot be true of God; because we call God the first efficient cause. Therefore, it is impossible that in God His existence should differ from His essence." *ST*, I.3.4.

God while still being *in* God. But how are things *in* God? God is a life of mutual giving and receiving between Father, Son, and Holy Spirit; to be *in* God is therefore to take part in the gift giving that the Trinity enacts. Everything not God, therefore, exists through *participation*. Any other way of construing creaturely existence "perforce reserves a territory independent of God. The latter can lead only to nihilism (though in different guises). Participation, however, refuses any reserve of created territory, while allowing finite things their own integrity."[10]

Similarly, Barth notoriously rejects the presumption of natural theology that knowledge of God can be read from the knowledge of the world. "But always, when man has tried to read the truth from sun, moon and stars or from himself, the result has been an idol. But when God has been known and then known again in the world, so that the result was a joyful praise of God in creation, that is because He is to be sought and found by us in Jesus Christ."[11] We know God as Creator when we know that God has become human in Jesus of Nazareth. And lest all this sound Marcionite, we should remember that creation in the biblical account is not separate from the narrative of Israel's own creation and redemption. Adam's sin and the creation of Israel are continuous with the creation of the earth and sky. The first few chapters of Genesis, then, not only tell about the creation of the world but introduce the narrative about its redemption. For this reason Luke's gospel traces Jesus's genealogy back to Adam (3:13), and Paul characterizes Adam as a typological figure of Christ (Rom 5:14). Since the redemption brought in Christ cannot be understood without the creation of the people Israel, through whom all the nations of the world would be blessed, we must also say that we know God as Creator when we know that God has called Israel out of Egypt.

Robert Jenson provocatively, but I think rightly, speaks about the creation of Israel as a kind of incarnation of the Son in preexistence to Jesus in Bethlehem.[12] The narrative pattern of Israel's life is God's Son in this sense, just as Matthew's gospel narrates the holy family's return from Egypt in terms of the exodus (Matt 2:15). God the Son dwells with the world in Israel *as* the march toward the incarnation. The Son preex-

---

10. Milbank et al., "Suspending the Material," 3. In these sentences, these authors no doubt mean much more than I do here. For them, participation also applies to the academic disciplines whereby, for example, philosophy is a subset of theology.

11. Barth, *Dogmatics in Outline*, 52.

12. See esp. Jenson, *Systematic Theology*, 1:138–44.

ists the incarnation within the biblical narrative in such a way that he is nevertheless not unincarnate. For Jenson, following Barth, this must be so because if God is himself his decision (if his being is to act), then his decision to be with the world in Christ is not simply a move of agency as it would be for us, the choice of a self that exists independently of choosing. God's decision to be for us in Christ is rather the reality of a God who is himself Jesus the man, so the incarnation is a "presupposition" of the Son in eternity.[13] Two observations flow from this.

First, creation and redemption are held together by the identity of God's decision to create the world with God's decision to be with the world in Christ. These are not two decisions, but one, and as such make clear how the world exists *for* Christ, which is the claim in Colossians (1:16–17).[14] Creation is because of Christ (meaning *through* him) and therefore *for* Christ—this bears some elaboration. Does the Father merely create or merely redeem through the Son? The right answer to the question is that this is a false distinction between creation and redemption, and we need to clarify how it, in fact, constitutes a false distinction. Creation is not only in the past but is part of the present so long as there exists anything other than God. As we have already said, God's decision to create is not separable from his intention to be with his creation—both are accomplished by Christ. So long as creation exists, the Son has a mission to it, though this statement cannot be construed as either somehow about the demands internal to a created order or as God's psychologistic realization, *after he had created,* to send his Son to his creation. Rather the Son's mission to creation is already bound up with God's decision to create through the Son, as Barth argued. The way that creation is *for* Christ is itself Christ's mission (or it is perhaps better to say that it is nothing less than his mission, though it may certainly be more). God's free decision to create something out of nothing is also his decision to be with his creation in Christ. We wrongly separate creation from redemption when we think that the incarnation of Christ only restores the original creation rather than fulfills and completes it. But the kingdom of God is more than a return to the Garden of Eden; we are not just restored to Adam's early state but are promised something *new,* which Christ brings.[15] Christ

---

13. Jenson, *Systematic Theology,* 1:140.
14. The claim from Colossians will be discussed more below.
15. To be sure, a large theological discussion stands behind these remarks I will not take up here.

in creation *is* Christ in redemption; the Son who is God's speaking of a creative word is also God's speaking of a saving word. And the crucial insight is that these two words are the same, namely, Jesus the Christ.

Second, God's life as the narrative of Israel on the way to the Messiah is part of God's eternity. Here we may cite John Howard Yoder in an extraordinary observation that echoes Jenson's (and Barth's) point with precision:

> In the old debates about the Trinity, one of the ways of stating the question that Tertullian and Origen discussed was whether God was ever speechless. Was God ever without the *Logos?* The answer was: "No, God from eternity had the *Logos*." We must say essentially the same thing about temporality if we are to understand the biblical vision of history. We cannot conceive of an atemporal God reconcilable with the biblical vision of God. We can conceive of a hypertemporal God who is more temporal than we are, who is ahead of us and behind us, before us and after us, above us in several directions, and who has more the character of timeliness and meaningfulness in movement rather than less.[16]

The life of Jesus Christ is a life in the world, just as the preincarnate Son exists in the history of the world among a particular people's story in the Near East. And Christ's reign with the Father, resurrected and glorified, is likewise a part of his history. None is atemporal. Christians know this through the way that the Son exists to the church as the body of Christ. Such a presence is sacramental; but the reality of Israel's historic existence as God's Son is no less sacramental than the reality of the church, since both share in the same promise of God to be the God of a new people, though the church is itself the temple of God.[17]

I do not want to pretend to have dealt adequately with these questions. There is surely much more to say if we were to treat them systematically and exegetically.[18] I intend here, however, simply to make some illustrations of what I mean by saying that creation is God's continual presence to the world as much as of the world's beginning. In this I mean

---

16. Yoder, *Preface to Theology*, 276. I am grateful to Stanley Hauerwas for pointing out how much Yoder sounds like Jenson here. If only Jenson would read Yoder.

17. Just as Paul appropriates the Old Testament promise of God in 2 Cor 6:16.

18. For example, for a recent challenge to Jenson's notion of preexistence, see Crisp, "Robert Jenson on the Pre-existence of Christ," 27–45.

to suggest a fundamental connection between Christ and the natural world, or what Christians ought to call the created world. What is natural is not somehow apart from God, but in God. And creation is in God because of Christ. By not separating phases in the life of the Son and by not separating God's decision to create from God's decision to be for the world in Christ, I hope to have made room for the fact that, fundamentally, Christians confess that God did not just create magnificently, but tends gently. Creation does not name just an event in the past, but the ongoing process through which God upholds everything—big and small. The wonders of astrophysics remind us that the universe is exceedingly vast and dramatic. But if this is our Father's world, we are permitted even to give thanks for those whose daily work is to tend to creation. These ones remind us that the universe is made up of small, fragile things—all of which would die without God's tenderness. The confession of God as Creator is therefore also a prayer for ourselves, for the patience to tend insofar as our confession embraces the participation of God in divine creation.

So Christians should not be surprised to find themselves giving thanks for those whose work makes their hands dirty or bloody, knowing that stewards are servants. We may pray for farmers and day laborers (those whose toil brings us food), knowing that we cannot neglect them or assume that food comes quickly or easily. If this world belongs to God, we must bless those who plant, harvest, pick, and slaughter; those whose livelihoods are tied closely to the soil, the weather, watersheds, and insects. We must pray to God that we will live in peace with creation and believe that it not only is good but gives glory to God. In the words of that wonderful liturgical phrase from the Anglican *Common Worship*: "all your works echo the silent music of your praise."[19] If God does not only *create* the world but continues to *tend and uphold* it in love, we are right to focus on those people in our midst who need our tending: the sick, the depressed, the infirm, the lonely, the frail, the very young, and the very old. This, and so much more, Christians must understand as the meaning of the truth that this is our Father's world.

---

19. Archbishop's Council, *Common Worship*, 201.

## CHRIST AND CREATION

Despite what I have just stated and what I have borrowed from Barth and Jenson, it is underappreciated that creation is first of all a christological concept.[20] If Genesis tells us that God did the creating, then John's gospel gets much more specific. The New Testament confession of Christians is that creation ultimately belongs not to the Father but to the Son. Everything that exists, exists for and through Christ.

> All things came into being through him, and without him not one thing came into being. What has come into being in him was life, and the life was the light of all people. (John 1:3–4)

Not one thing came into being without the Son of God, which is also a theme found elsewhere in the New Testament:

> In him all things were created, in heaven and on earth, visible and invisible, whether thrones or dominions or principalities or authorities—all things were created through him and for him. He is before all things, and in him all things hold together. (Col 1:16–17)

The Son of God is not only the agent of creation—the way God created everything that exists—but also the one we may now identify as continuing to uphold and tend what he created.

The Son of God is begotten, not made, which means that he is not a part of creation. He is not "the crown of all creation" as humanity is, neither is he *made* in the image of God, though he *is* the image of God. These are admittedly careful distinctions. God as Trinity eternally exists amid reciprocating speech of mutual obligation, of antiphonal command and response in obedience. However, as Jenson argues, the speech that creates is itself a command that is already moral. It takes the form of "Let there be . . ." to which creation obediently responds by coming into being.[21] Therefore, the pronouncement that "it is good" is likewise a moral judgment on the obedience of creation to the word of God's creative speech. Creation is moral simply in virtue of its existence. This is the meaning of

---

20. For a historical account of why the role of Christ in creation was diminished after Irenaeus, see Gunton, "Doctrine of Creation," 141–57.

21. Jenson, *Systematic Theology*, 2:27. This, of course, should not be construed to mean that the world creates itself. Its speech cannot be a first act but only a reply in which such speech is *given* by God and *received* by the world—received in its being offered back to God.

the ubiquity of goodness that Augustine derives in his argument for evil as privation.[22] Insofar as anything exists, good exists, since existence is a good; evil can have no independent, positive *existence* since in having existence it would by necessity be good, which it is not. The total absence of good thus formally equates to nonbeing, that is, to the total absence of existence, which, obviously, is nothing, and which certainly is not an existence of evil. This argument makes utterly unfathomable the thought (Manichaean or otherwise) about matter's being evil.

And, as we have said, the Son is how God creates the world. The Son is the Logos, the eternal Word of God, who is God's creative speech in the command for the world to come into existence. As Jenson puts it, "God speaks a moral command to create the world. The moral command that he speaks is the Son."[23] Still, we surely more commonly think about creation as an *event* and, therefore, as amoral rather than moral. Things that exist in time may be contingently related to other historical facts, but they do not usually submit to judgments about good and bad. We may assert that this or that past event caused happiness or sorrow, joy or pain; and indeed we and others may still be living with these things in our memories. Is this the kind of moral event creation is? In the first example (creation as event), to make a moral judgment seems to be a category mistake; in the second (the moral weight of our happiness or sorrow, of our joy or pain), such a judgment seems warranted or at least nearer the mark.

Nevertheless the moral act of creation still differs from the latter example. Creation is not simply an event in the past, since the present is as much created as the past is. Only so long as creation is conceived of as a mere past event can we think that it has no (or very little) purchase on the present. Rejecting this, though, carries the implication that there can therefore be no memory of creation; it is not a part of anyone's experience but is the condition of possibility for all experience. At issue is not just that creation produced no witnesses, but that it is of an entirely different order compared to witnessable events.[24] And if there can be no memory

---

22. As found in *Confessions* 7.18.
23. Jenson, *Systematic Theology*, 2:27.
24. John Polkinghorne makes the same point if perhaps with an injudicious partiality to the story science tells about the origins of the universe in *Faith of a Physicist*, ch. 4.

of the creation, there can be no judgments made at the level of the joy or pain it produced for us or others.[25]

The distinction named by the creedal confession that the Son was "begotten" and "not made" is held open with the same logic that establishes a difference between God and creation *through the speech that enacts creation*. And it is not just the same logic but is, in fact, the same thing in every respect. Barth argued as much:

> It is impossible to separate the knowledge of God the Creator and of His work from the knowledge of God's dealings with *man*. Only when we keep before us what the triune God has done for us men in Jesus Christ can we realize what is involved in God the Creator and His work. Creation is the temporal analogue, taking place outside God, of that event in God Himself by which God is the Father of the Son. The world is not God's Son, is not "begotten" of God; but it is *created*. But what God does as the Creator can in the Christian sense only be seen and understood as a reflection, as a shadowing forth of this inner divine relationship between God the Father and the Son.[26]

One important aspect of this distinction is that humanity relates to the Father differently than the Son. The reason we say "Abba, Father" is different (though not entirely different) from the reason Jesus Christ does. The Son is eternally the Son of the Father, forever speaking "Father" in an unbroken fellowship that is itself nothing other than what it means for God to be God. In other words, as Augustine expounded in *De Trinitate*, God is the eternal existence of the Father and Son in eternal relationship with each other in the Holy Spirit. It is different for us because we are not members of the Trinity. We belong to Christ through creation, and so our very existence glorifies God.

We belong to the Father, not as begotten sons and daughters, but as *adopted* siblings to our brother Jesus Christ. We are brought into the family of God through the work of redemption.[27] Christians have been

---

25. The lament "I wish I had never been born" comes close to a regret for creation. Even so, "creation" does not refer primarily to the appearance of individual entities, and so, insofar as the speaking subject ("I") speaks or thinks or feels even regret, such speaking, thinking, and feeling is still good in some measure since it is part of creation.

26. Barth, *Dogmatics in Outline*, 52.

27. Which, as before, raises a question against drawing strong distinctions between creation and redemption.

adopted by the Father to be able to call Christ brother, and this is on account of the resurrection. As Colossians reminds us, creation exists *for* him. He is not only the agent of creation but the *recipient* of creation, which means that the praise of creation *is* the worship of the Son. Since creation belongs to him, so also does creation's praise. This includes the conscious praise of those who knowingly adore the Son of God with their bodies and lives, but it also includes the silent praise of the rocks that cry out, the declarations of the stars concerning the glory of God. It is easy to sentimentalize those things that praise God in this way: a dog's joy, a tree's uplifted branches, a child's laughter. Nevertheless naming them as praise is a crucial task for those whose lives are shaped by an awareness of the Son's centrality to creation's praise. Put strongly, only those who can see trees as existing by and for the Son worship the Son themselves in truth. Our failure so to see is correlative of our inability to know the Son as the risen Lord.

## KNOWING THE EARTH

"Man exists, not in himself, but for God."[28] As human beings are drawn into the inner Trinitarian life of God, they become more fully participants in God's intention for creation, which is to say that they become more fully *themselves*. In the same way, the more we know about Christ, the more insight we will have into our world. The better we are at loving Christ, the better we will be at loving this world. After all, it is not an idle question to ask where we ought to turn in order to know how best to care for the natural world. In his devastating repudiation of ecotheologies like that of Sallie McFague, John Milbank observes a contemporary predilection for turning "back" to nature to discover the secrets of, say, its own harmony.[29] However, as Milbank argues, letting nature set the ethic for care of nature assumes that nature is relatively simple and obviously readable, that it is possible to know what "the whole" requires. But claims to have discovered what is most needful—optimum balances, recommended

---

28. Michael Schmaus, *Katholische Dogmatic* II, 70–72, quoted in von Balthasar, *Theology of Karl Barth*, 349–50.

29. Milbank, *Word Made Strange*, ch. 11. An example of McFague's catastrophic theology can be found in *Models of God*, esp. ch. 3, which posits "the world as God's body." Thankfully, she begins by calling it "a bit of nonsense" (ibid., 69). Rowan Williams asks whether propositions like McFague's entail "an uncritical maternal image to replace an uncritical patriarchal image?" (*On Christian Theology*, 78).

levels of consumption matched by simply derived carbon offsets, and so on—can too easily conceal the designs of human power that supervene and motivate these claims.[30] And the issue is not only human corruption, as this obtains neither more nor less in this sphere than in others. More important, the issue is the unchecked assumption that something called "nature" exists independently of what human culture imagines to correspond to that nomenclature. So long as we think of nature as an objective reality, we will potentially fail to see how the requirements incumbent on our care of it are actually artifacts of our ideas of what it means for nature to be natural.

But if nature is natural on account of grace, as I have been arguing, then our knowledge of it will of necessity be theological. This conclusion may seem something of a letdown. But it is not meant to be the bald assertion of theology over the other disciplines, as if there might be what Heidegger mockingly referred to as "Protestant mathematics." I do not mean "theology" in a strict sense, but as a stance, a mode of perception that sees the world in God and nothing outside of God. I mean for this conclusion to do some constructive work as a proposal, rather than as an abstract and merely theoretical *quod erat demonstrandum* as vulnerable to ideological perversion as the atheistic naturalism it opposes. The world is vast and the natural world extraordinarily complex. Appealing to God is not a silver bullet that promises to solve it all or render it comprehensible.

In fact, a theological conception of nature holds open precisely the possibility that we might find the grace to live in a world that we cannot fully understand or bring under our control. In modern times, where the biblical idea of human "dominion" has been rejected and made to take the blame for environmental disorder, it not only has been misunderstood, but has also likely functioned as a ruse for human power. After all, with the loss of a Christian account of human dominion over nature, we have undoubtedly witnessed a simple substitution of one form of dominion for another. As Colin Gunton puts it,

> If we cease to see the world as God's creation, we shall treat it not as a project [of God's] in which we are invited to share but as an absolute possession to be exploited as we will.[31]

---

30. Ibid., 262.
31. Gunton, "Doctrine of Creation," 155.

It is not at all clear that technology can save us in this regard. Technologies once thought successful are declared disasters when additional factors are discovered that were not found within the original purview. For example, Paul Virilio observes that every invention is also the invention of an accident: the invention of the locomotive contains within itself the invention of the derailment; the invention of the stock market contains the invention of the stock market crash; the ship, the shipwreck; and so on. If we do not normally think in these terms, Virilio says, it is because the very discourse of technology prevents us from doing so, by serving to separate us from real events. (He is thinking mostly of how the "world" portrayed on television makes the real world invisible to us.) But this only makes us stupid and does nothing to dampen our hope in technology's promise to save us from a dangerous world "out there" that is full of accidents.[32] I take this to mean that the complexity of the natural world is never a known quantity matched by technology, even though we are doomed to believe assurances that it is. Better technologies will therefore *always* emerge as they are refined and adapted to meet our ever-growing awareness of the world's complexity. Yet if Virilio is right, we cannot help but suspect that our new knowledge is risibly insignificant in view of this complexity. Our technologies either will finally not be able to keep pace with our knowledge or else, even if they do, will always therefore be just as inadequate as our knowledge—just as small, and suffering equally from our overestimation and arrogance. Therefore, technology may only further our estrangement from God insofar as it cannot come to terms with its limited mode of knowledge.

What we need, Milbank suggests, is "a civil knowledge not currently available."[33] He surely has in mind a variation on a theological worldview that has been replaced by secularism. The overestimation that places hope in technology is a secular, civil way of being, insofar as it establishes a *telos* for human community with a severely foreshortened reach, a set of concerns easily brought within the human political imagination that refuses to envision a complexity beyond its own potential for management. What is the alternative? Without claiming to know what would be required to make such knowledge civil, let me nevertheless offer some idea of what this alternative knowledge might look like.

---

32. See Virilio, *Original Accident*.
33. Milbank, *Word Made Strange*, 266.

First, the world is no more complex than God. This may be either reassuring or exasperating depending on the knowledge we hope to have of it. It is not to be confused with the orthodox affirmation of God's simplicity, which refers to God's not having parts rather than to the ease with which he is apprehended. Indeed, in this regard, divine simplicity *is part of his complexity* insofar as we have no knowledge or experience of anything else that is simple (since nothing created has simplicity, divine or otherwise). But knowing and living in a complex world will require the skill of a people who have learned to live before a complex God.[34]

Second, such a life will be marked by uncertainty. Uncertainty, of course, but names a chastened knowledge that has come to terms with complexity. It is not a first principle, a metaphysical statement about the inherent chaos of existence: *complexity* is metaphysical; uncertainty is not.[35] Nevertheless God's freedom will not let us approach his creation in any other way than with wonder at mysteries that we cannot manage or solve. So long as our rationalism keeps us from admitting that God is a mystery, we will overestimate our certainty by underestimating the complexity of our reason's objects. Living with uncertainty will mean accepting the fact that we do not control what is natural through our knowledge of nature, which means that if there is such a thing as "natural knowledge," it will always be deeper than our descriptions.

Third, life in a complex world will be guided by promise. The kind of knowledge Christians have of God is not named by possession but by promise. God's very name, the unspeakable YHWH, is more basic to our knowledge of him than the label "God" since we cannot claim to know what a "God" is apart from the name. Nevertheless, folks claim to know "God" all the time. It can be easy to assume that God is a univocal category that potentially admits of a variety of names. Then once we find

---

34. Though this makes me sympathetic with theories of intelligent design, I am suspicious of the tendency of those working in that area to make complexity *prove* something. My own expectations would be much more humble in this respect, especially where the public voice of the movement makes apologetic use of complexity for arguing the existence of a creator. It seems, rather, that an awareness of complexity means more for the task of chastening the aims of science, technology, public works, medicine, and so on than it does for proving God's existence, which, as I have been arguing, is bound up with the worship of God as creator.

35. As metaphysical or ontological avowals, only complexity can be theological since it is rooted in God whereas *uncertainty*, an epistemological term with the ontological analogue *chaos*, can only ever be pagan.

out his name, we simply attach that name to the concept we have already had for God. This is surely idolatry—fitting God within a prior human category; which means that having God's name can be an obstacle to faith in God since it can tempt us to tie God down with it. Still, God's very name, YHWH, resists our grasping because it is itself God's promise to be present to Israel. God's name and identity are wrapped up with his promise to fulfill himself to his people. "This is my name forever" (Exod 3:15) is God's promise to be Israel's God forever, just as God's name *is itself that very promise*.[36] And this is why God's name is not to be spoken. By the name's not being spoken, its status as promise is respected in acknowledgement that it cannot be possessed. But why not? Because to possess God's name would be to possess God's promise. And what might it mean to *possess* a promise? Once you possess a promise, you no longer have a need for the promise-maker. But God's promise is precisely the ongoing presence of the promise-maker to his people. Therefore, if God's name could be possessed, there would be no promise since God would be dead. Put simply, then, to name God is to court the temptation to grasp at the promise and, in so doing, to kill God. Christian knowledge of God is Jewish in this regard and is extended in this logic on account of the resurrection, itself an act of promise to remain with the sinful world on the way to redemption. Our knowledge is animated by trust, belief that the promises of God are true, that the word God spoke to us in Christ is genuine, and that a resurrected Christ is a deeper reality than we can comprehend.

Therefore, our speech—the stuff of our knowledge—differs from God's. Jenson observes that God's address can be declaration since he has power over the future, which is the power to fulfill the promises he makes. But within the promises of God's declaration, we speak as questioners precisely on account of our inability to possess the future.[37] Put differently, the future belongs only to God through promise. If we can only live with the complexity of the world in view of the world's open future in which we are included, we give ourselves as participants in conversation with the God who holds the future open for the world through promise: the history of the world is the temporal gap between promise

---

36. And again we should recall Paul's appropriation of the promise to the church in 2 Cor 6:16.

37. Jenson, *Systematic Theology*, 2:64.

and fulfillment.[38] This act of holding open the promise and of conversing during it is called "creation."

In a rapid though admittedly elliptical fashion, we have returned to the problem of complexity. If the world is no more complex than God and God is known by his promise, which is his very name and the reality of the resurrection, then knowledge of what is "natural" will have the form of believing promise. Put differently, the faith required to trust that God has purposes for creation beyond our own making is no different from the faith necessary to have natural knowledge. When we know what is "natural" as "creation," we know it better. And just as such faith is not a static comportment or a fixed quantity enumerable and describable in abstract or *a priori* terms, so also knowledge of nature is bound up with the continuing movement of creature with Creator. It is a relational knowledge, based not on pantheistic claims about the life of the (living, breathing) earth or on the divinity of creation, but on the enclosure of all creation within the life of God. Creation is not sacred; God is. Sharing in divine knowledge is the faith to accept God's providence over creation as distinct from it and yet as fully present to it in every respect.

Those who believe God's promises know God as promise-maker in worship. The movement from nature to creation is traversed by love since as God's creatures our worship is nothing other than love of our Creator. The vision of a people who so love, formed in worship, enables them to see things as they truly are. We know more fully what the meaning of the earth is by making sacramental use of the wheat and grapes that it produces. Our vision is renewed in the sanctuary of God. We know better by faith than by sight because there is more to see than we can see. This is not only because of what we usually think of as "unseen things," but also because seeing in faith attunes us to the objects of knowledge that would remain hidden without it. This can never be a knowledge that grasps and controls, that "knows" completely or denies freedom to the objects of that knowledge. It is a knowledge that awaits surprise, that attends to the free possibility of unexpected things, and that refuses to presume that collecting information about dead things by tearing them apart can ever count as knowledge.[39] This knowledge knows God as Creator in the pres-

---

38. As von Balthasar argues in *Theology of History*, 127–33.
39. I do not mean to malign the many accomplishments of modern biology, but I sus-

ent tense and looks for and finds his handiwork everywhere. When it does so, it is never ultimately alarmed, but it is always surprised.

---

pect this is why it is ill equipped ever to discover what life truly is. Instead it is likely only ever to confirm its theories in this respect according to its naturalistic presumptions. I am sure that many biologists have "respect for life," but if they do, it is not a virtue they have been afforded through the discipline of biology (or medicine).

# PROCLAIMING

CHAPTER 8

*How Free Are We?**

TEXTS: 1 Kings 19:15–16, 19–21; Psalm 16;
Galatians 5:1, 13–18; Luke 9:51–62

I

How free are we?

Of course a lot depends on who is asking the question. A philosopher who asks it may be wondering if anything we do is really free, or if it is all just determined. A politician who asks it may want us to consider who we are as a nation and what it means to be free from oppression.

In modern times, there is almost nothing better we can think of than being free. Just think about the freedom of choice. What could be better than the ability to choose freely? Nothing. In fact, choice has become *so* great that it has even become better than anything you could possibly choose. Choice itself is better than anything you could possibly get through exercising your choice.

We would rather keep our options open. We are scared to death that something better might always come along. It's the logic behind the recent controversial billboard in Chicago for a law firm: the billboard showed beautiful male and female bodies and read, "Life is short; get a divorce." It may sound absurd, but choice is now better than anything else.

You may think I am kidding. But what do we call someone who would rather be a free chooser than be satisfied with having made a choice? We call that person a *consumer*. And we are all consumers much of the time. Our lives can be so wrapped up with consuming that we hardly notice it. Is your music collection so big that nothing you listen to can be quite as impressive as the bigness of your collection? Is your

---

* A sermon preached on July 1, 2007.

television so flat and high-definition that you are still on the lookout for the perfect movie to watch on it? Is your sound system so "surround" that your music and DVDs simply can't measure up? We become dissatisfied with the choices we have made because we would rather have choice *before* us, not *behind* us. We would rather be on the brink of choosing than having just chosen.

It is to us, then, as American consumers that the Word of the Lord comes today. We can think of nothing better than being free. But the message of the God of Elijah and Elisha, of Abraham, Moses, and Jesus is radically different. It is that we are only free when we are yoked to what is true.

Of course, we tend to think that being free means not being yoked to *anything at all*. Throw off the shackles, burn the draft cards or the bras or the books or the flags . . . anything that holds us back. Push ahead into an unbounded future. Free! Not tied to the past. Not tied to anything.

In today's Scripture reading, we get a sense of this kind of freedom. God tells Elijah that it is time to appoint his successor, and he is told who it will be. Elijah is to go find a man called Elisha and appoint him to be a prophet. And so he finds Elisha plowing in his fields, and then the scene turns a little bit dramatic. Elijah issues the call and Elisha wants to say goodbye to his parents. That seems pretty normal. But when he returns, Elisha makes a remarkable display of his break with the past. He throws off his burden of plowing the fields, burns the yokes, and eats his oxen! There will be no more work for Elisha. He is now free.

## II

The story of America tells a version of this kind of freedom. It is a story of freedom *from*: It is a story of freedom from tyranny, from oppression, from foreign rule. America isn't too upset with the British anymore, but we all know about the time when Britain was the tyrant and America suffered for want of freedom. In the eighteenth and nineteenth centuries, at the height of *their* Empire, Britons sang "Rule, Britannia! Britannia, rule the waves. Britons never shall be slaves." That is a rousing chorus for those who can sing it. But Britannia would not have ruled the waves if it had not been so good at making other people slaves. The port at Liverpool was the Heathrow Airport of the nineteenth century, through which passed an abundant slave trade.

America too is full of contradictions—not only about its own history of slavery, but also in its struggle for freedom against foreign occupation. Sometimes we like to think that because of how this story goes, we Americans are actually quite a bit like other native peoples around the world who are also under foreign rule. We identify with them in their opposition to a colonizing power, whether it is former Soviet republics, India (another former British colony), or relatively new African nations who have recently found freedom from European imperialism.

But actually, America could not be more different. After all, it was not the Native Americans who threw out the colonizing British, but the colonists themselves, who were so good at colonizing that they no longer needed the mother country. Colonialism was not *overturned* in the American story; it was *confirmed*. It worked *too* well.[1] We need to be reminded: there was no American equivalent to Gandhi.

Even so, it is inscribed in our national psyche that freedom is about choice and self-determination. It is of such importance that it justifies and even requires violent revolution in order to secure it. The line between who we are as *consumers* and as *fighters* is, therefore, not one that is easily drawn.

Yet this is the story of America. All of this is what it means for America to be free; and we celebrate it on the Fourth of July.

### III

But we are Christians. We have a different story. And it is a decidedly different story of freedom. America's story is one of victory for colonizers who sought self-determination through violent revolution. The Christian story is one of giving up power, of self-renunciation, and non-violent suffering.

And if America's story is freedom *from*, the Christian story is freedom *for*. It is freedom *for* obedience and service. It is not the casting off of every yoke, but only submitting to the yoke that is true. True freedom is perfect obedience. It is not about refusing to follow anyone but myself, but about following the one who created the universe and upholds it in love.

---

1. Even though this is obvious, I owe my awareness of this point to Lewis, "Revolt of Islam."

It is true that Elisha makes a break with the past. He is like the disciples Jesus calls at the edge of the lake, who drop their nets. They break with their fisherman pasts. But the life of a prophet, like the life of a disciple, is not a life of freedom in any straightforward sense. After all, at the end of our Scripture reading, we are told that Elisha has become a servant.

In three days America will celebrate its story. But today we celebrate the Christian story. We are gathered, not on the *first* day of the week, but on the *eighth* day, the day of the new creation, of the new age. It begins at dawn with the rising of the Son of God. The world has fundamentally and irrevocably changed.

On the Fourth of July, we will be told that we are free and that our freedom was "bought with a price," the blood of soldiers. In the celebration of this feast laid out before us, we are reminded that our freedom as Christians was also bought, but with a different price. We do not celebrate one who fought for freedom and died in the process, but one who *refused* to fight and died in the process.

As we partake of the body and blood of Christ, we are also reminded that we are not free. Jesus did not secure our freedom in the American sense. He did not promise that we would not be ruled by tyrants. He did not promise that our pasts would have no control over us. He did not promise us security or welfare. He did not even promise life, liberty, or the pursuit of happiness. In short, Jesus does not offer salvation on the American model.

Jesus *did* make promises to those who decided to follow him, but they were often grim. His own fate, of course, was grim. On this side of the resurrection, we can easily forget that the path of obedience does not go around the cross, but through it. And we must walk through it. This is why we *eat* Jesus's body and *drink* his blood rather than just look at pictures. We cannot stand at a distance; we *partake*, we *ingest*, we *digest*. And as the early Christians often remarked, eating this meal is unlike every other meal: everything else we eat becomes part of us; but when we eat this meal, we become part of what we eat. We celebrate the death of Jesus, but we also share in it. And we do not just share in its benefits but also in its horrors. The way of Jesus is not only the way of salvation but also the way of death.

Therefore, when we share in this feast, we are made part of a people we did not choose. We may have friends in church, but we are not here because we are friends. Instead, God has called us his friends and has made us members of one another because we share the same bread. You may not particularly like the person in the pew next to you, but so what? This is not the Kiwanis club, but a body God has called and assembled. We are not friends; we are brothers and sisters. As you know, brothers and sisters may fight, but no one can change the fact that they have the same father.

And we are not just one with each other here in this place, but with Christians all around the globe and throughout time. God's people are not bounded by national borders, cultural heritage, or language. If national boundaries keep us from the unity we share in this bread and cup, we disgrace this bread and cup. When culture and language get in the way of acknowledging our common calling as children of God, we are saying that we would rather be American than Christian. But God has made this people, and so we are not free to choose each other.

Furthermore, we may *choose* to follow Christ, but despite how we are otherwise made to think, *that choice* is better than choice itself. Choosing Christ is better than choice itself. So we do not follow Christ as consumers. When we begin to follow, we actually give up some choices that were formerly available to us. And that is good news! It is more blessed to be a disciple than a consumer. At baptism we gave up our freedom to self-determination. We no longer stand before a future in which we can do whatever we want. Instead we are open to a future that we cannot anticipate and that we are powerless to control. Elisha burned the yokes and ate the oxen—not only was there no going back, but there was now no going forward as before. The life of a prophet is not one of freedom but of radical obedience.

One thing the early Christians knew was that, as Christians, they were no longer free to die as they chose. How could they? They were partakers of someone else's death, sharers of someone else's death, die-ers of someone else's death. Your death and my death now only have meaning within the death of Christ. What would it mean for us to be a people who know it is not up to us to say how we die? We know this is a serious question in a culture where the dying are still consumers. Jack Kevorkian is on parole. Choice, freedom—even in death. What could be better?

## IV

So how free *are* we—not as Americans but as Christians? Not very, it seems. Put it this way: Would you have eaten Elisha's oxen? Would you have joined in that feast? Elisha's was the celebration of the past. The bodies of the beasts of burden became part of the bodies of those who gathered to wish Elisha *bon voyage*. We can't help but think that Elisha's feast was a kind of Fourth of July barbecue: The future is open, full of promise; thank God for the past.

You may recall that when would-be disciples wanted to go say goodbye to *their* loved ones, Jesus dismissed them. (That text from Luke's gospel is paired with this text about Elisha in today's lectionary.) This feast to which God himself has invited his people is a feast of new yokes. It is not the celebration of an unbounded future—of *no* yokes—but of a decidedly *bounded* future. We who share in it are yoked to one another because we become a part of what we eat and drink. We become part of a body that we are not the head of. We therefore do not celebrate the Lord's Supper lightly. We must count the cost. Those who eat of this table give up freedoms. What could possibly convince us to do that?

The gospel, of course, *does* have something to do with freedom. But it is terrible and frightening and wonderful. It haunts us because it is a mystery that we reject with nearly our entire beings. And it is also almost impossible for us to imagine it: that fighting for self-determination only entrenches our slavery; but as partakers of the bread of life, we are made free. Jesus refused to fight and was killed in the process. But the secret is that his refusal to fight *is* our freedom. We are only free when we are yoked to what is true. The bread of life, the body of Christ, is the true yoke.

This is a terrifying kind of freedom. And we celebrate it and enact it in a way that the world can only call bizarre. This freedom is not obviously joyful, immediately rewarding, or intuitively satisfying. When looked at against the background of America's story of freedom, it is very difficult to see. But it is the only gospel I know. God help us to see it.

CHAPTER 9

*Basking and Speaking in Ordinary Time*\*

TEXTS: Jeremiah 1:4–10; Acts 2:1–7; Psalm 71:1–6

I

Some people never can escape from the academic calendar. For them, it is fall rather than spring that is full of new beginnings. Spring is the time to finish things up. And for them, summer is not just a time of activity in the sun, but also a time of waiting. The academic calendar has a great pause for a few months in the summer, and for those who live by it, it can even come to feel like a bore after a while.

Now, for those who pay attention to such things, the Christian calendar actually seems to allow us to feel a little bored during the summer months. The church calls this period "Ordinary Time." It's the period between Trinity Sunday in June and Christ the King Sunday in November. That's quite a long summer for the church. What are we supposed to do during that time? Just wait? That doesn't seem quite right: after all, once things start up again, we'll quickly pass into the season of Advent, which is *really* about waiting. There's nothing more dispiriting than waiting to wait. So what should we be doing during Ordinary Time?

Let me tell you what I propose. I propose that we *bask*. Let us, in Ordinary Time, bask. And why not bask in the gifts we have received from God in the last few weeks before we found ourselves in Ordinary Time? We had Pentecost and Trinity Sunday. And so let us bask in the Holy Spirit that comes into the world and creates the church at Pentecost. And why not bask in the glory of the Holy Trinity that we celebrated mere

---

\* A sermon preached on August 26, 2007.

weeks ago? These are things that cannot be contained by, or celebrated, or basked in for just one week. We need all summer to do it.

God the Holy Spirit has created a new people out of the nations of the world, has given himself to it in gift and speech, has promised forgiveness to us and our reconciliation to one another. The glory of Pentecost is not just an event but a whole program for our existence as that new people. The Holy Spirit is the one Jesus promised to send, the one who would not only walk beside us but, as we have read, will infiltrate our very mouths and speech. We bear an extraordinary mission and have been given everything we need to carry it out. That's the glory of Pentecost.

Now Jesus sits enthroned in heaven receiving praises day and night. Not just from us, but with the heavenly host of angels and archangels, who ceaselessly sing about the worth of the Lamb to receive glory. And we do not just sing about giving him glory; we actually do it. This is Jesus the Christ who lives and reigns with God the Father and the Holy Spirit in loving and eternal communion, in perfect harmony of giving and receiving. We barely know what we are talking about when we talk about the Holy Trinity. These words we use, we also know, fail to do justice to the wonder of God's glory as he exists in inexhaustible splendor and beauty. The most truthful thing we can do, then, is bask in it all. Let the sweetness of God's goodness and everlasting presence sweep over us. Breathe in the warmth of the love between the Father and the Son, a warmth that we share in as creatures whose acceptance by God *is* the love between the Father and the Son.

Extraordinary, isn't it? There's almost too much of this stuff. There's certainly enough to roll around in for a few months. Ordinary Time is anything but ordinary.

II

But all of this bliss is potentially shattered by God's abrupt command to go and speak. Speak? How could we possibly do that? Our lips and tongues are still numb with the grandeur of it all. We barely know what we have witnessed. How could we possibly tell anyone about it?

You and I normally speak out of our pride. And I don't just mean that we speak about ourselves most of the time, although we do. We speak out of our pride when the confidence that drives us to speak comes from our confidence in our understanding. No one wants to speak only to look foolish and be told, "You have no idea what you are talking about." We don't actually have to know what we're saying in order to speak, of course; we say stupid things all the time. But that just means that our confidence in what we say often outpaces what we're actually saying. That's pride.

And it might seem that our speaking about God is really no different. After all, we are commanded to say things that we do not actually understand. Our words are inherently inadequate.

But the difference is that our pride normally serves up our words even if we are about to say something stupid. But the words about God come from God. God touches Jeremiah's mouth, giving him words. The Holy Spirit descends on fearful apostles giving them tongues of fire: a new way of speaking, new words, a new confidence. They do not speak because they have understood it all—how could they?

Consider the fact that Christian art has generally refrained from depicting the resurrection in any form. A painting may show the empty tomb or the glorious, risen Christ. But Christian artists have shied away from trying to depict the act of the resurrection itself; and the Gospels do the same thing. How could we talk about something that we cannot comprehend? We do, of course, find ways of talking about the resurrection, but our pride is chastened by them since we fundamentally do not really know what a resurrection is.

And so the reason we still talk about the resurrection is the same reason that Jeremiah was a prophet and why twelve disciples became apostles. It is that this speech is itself a gift of God.

But we need to be clear about one thing. The word of God is entrusted to his church, not just to individuals. We can be tempted to read these texts as though we as individuals receive private words from God. Of course God speaks in a variety of ways, but his Holy Spirit does not reside in individuals but in the church. In the New Testament, we read about the Holy Spirit descending on two crucial occasions: on Jesus at his baptism and on the church at Pentecost. And these are not very different from each other. If the church is the body of Christ, then on both occasions we see the Holy Spirit being united with Christ.

But we don't want the Holy Spirit to be united *with Christ*; we want the Holy Spirit to be united with *the individual*. How often have Christians been told that your individual body is the temple of the Holy Spirit, when in fact it is the church that is the temple of the Holy Spirit? It is not my individual body or your individual body. When Paul asks in 1 Corinthians

6:19, "Do you not know that your body is a temple of the Holy Spirit?" he is speaking in the plural. He is saying, do y'all not know that your body is the temple of the Holy Spirit? "Y'all" is plural; "body" is singular. So what is y'all's body? It is the body of Christ, the church.

This is why we celebrate two things simultaneously at Pentecost: the creation of the church by the Holy Spirit and the gift of the Holy Spirit to that church. These two things are really one. The word of God that is given to the church *is* the creation of the church.

Now I'm aware that that will sound a bit strange. Or maybe you just think that this is the kind of stuff theologians busy themselves with—and I can tell you, it surely is. But here is what all of this means. The glory of God—basked in, soaked up—despite everything else, *can* be spoken about. And here is why: *Because the telling of the glory is part of the glory.* We do not just tell of God's glorious works; instead, our telling of them is itself also a glorious work of God.

If we insist on speaking about God out of our pride, out of our understanding, it will not be God we are speaking about. God does not meet our ignorance with understanding, enabling us to speak. Instead God meets our confusion with confidence.

### III

But there is another reason we have for not speaking. If the first is the inadequacy of our speech about God, the second is our reluctance for fear of being misunderstood. And this is a real fear. Jeremiah is not guaranteed to be understood when he speaks to the nations. The apostles, it is true, surprise the gathered crowds when they are understood far more widely than anyone could have ever thought. But if you know the story of Acts, you know they will meet with resistance soon enough. Reluctance at being misunderstood can drive us to silence.

My wife and I lived in England for three years. We were always amused when people would remind us of George Bernard Shaw's famous statement that "England and America are two countries separated by a common language." There is something deceptive about taking comfort in the fact that we could continue to speak English in this foreign place. Of course we could still speak English in England. But I'll tell you, I've never felt so aware that the language I *really* speak is Californian. I am sure that my California English must have grated on old world ears.

I found myself becoming quieter, more reluctant. I hesitated more before speaking, and then, when I did speak, I spoke less. The problem was not that I had less to say. I was not uncertain of my words in that sense. But I was often unsure of how my words would be received, whether I had chosen the right words, and what my speaking would reveal about me without me really being aware of it.

Jeremiah is called by God to be a prophet to the nations. He was not just asked to speak to his own people, but in foreign lands to foreign people. He objects to God that he does not know how to speak. He cannot speak with eloquence or authority because, as he says in protest, "I am only a boy." And the apostles who burst out of the upper room proclaiming the good news about Jesus? "Are they not Galileans? Those are fishing villages up there, right? Not halls of learning. Why should we listen to them?"

Well, that's a good question. Why does God choose these people? Why choose Moses, who protested similar things? Why put the message of Jesus in the hands of uneducated fishermen? Why entrust the witness of the resurrection of Jesus to women who, simply for being women at that time in history, bore a testimony that would not hold up in court?

Why does God choose these people? For no other reason than the very reason we object to them: they are unbelievable. They don't possess any qualities that would commend them to us as authorities. The only authority they have is the truth of the message they bear. We do not have to listen to them; they can't hurt us if we refuse them; they can't shame us if we don't believe what they say. They are weak. That's why God chooses them.

We need to remember: God's message to the nations is *God's* message. We are all familiar with what happens when the message goes forth with force, with the strength of armies behind it, with credentials that shame unbelievers into belief. When that happens, it is not God's message, but ours. And it certainly can't be a message about a suffering servant, about a king that allows himself to be killed.

The reluctance of the weak who are still called to bear a seemingly unbelievable message is not met with strength in any straightforward sense. It is met with the promise that the God of the message is alive in the world and goes ahead of the church. When the message carried by a weak church is rejected, at least the message is not corrupted by those who witness to it. It becomes more likely that the world is actually responding to the gospel, even when it rejects the gospel. And that's good. Let's be sure the world rejects the *gospel*. In a world where truth and force seem to go together, what could be more natural than rejecting the words of the weak?

Many of us, of course, are not weak. People will listen to some of us no matter what we say. And historically the church has not always been weak. But then we shouldn't be surprised when God makes us listen to our brothers and sisters from Galilee, to fishermen, or worse. And we shouldn't be surprised if God is making the church in America weaker. It has had too many swords and too few nets. We are not guaranteed that our speech will be understood, but sometimes that can only make us impatient—impatient with weakness.

## IV

Which is why we need Ordinary Time so badly. We are asked to wait with patience. We have been given a time to chasten our proud words, to allow God to penetrate our confusion, and meet our reluctance with his promise to the weak. And most of all, it is a time to bask.

As long as Christians don't know how to bask in the glory of God, the world will remain unconvinced by what Christians say about God. We are not very good at basking. That is why we don't trust God, why we justify our violence, why we are ashamed of weakness and of the cross of Christ, and why we would rather be silent than proclaim. But thank God for this extraordinary, ordinary time.

BIBLIOGRAPHY

Adams, Nicholas. "Reasoning in Tradition." In *The Blackwell Companion to Christian Ethics*, edited by Stanley Hauerwas and Samuel Wells, 209–22. Blackwell Companions to Religion. Oxford: Blackwell, 2004.

Aquinas, Thomas. *Summa Theologica*. 5 vols. Translated by Fathers of the English Dominican Province. Allen, TX: Christian Classics, 1981.

Archbishop's Council of the Church of England. *Common Worship: Services and Prayers for the Church of England*. London: Church House, 2000.

Arendt, Hannah. *Crises of the Republic*. New York: Harcourt Brace, 1972.

Ariès, Philippe. *Western Attitudes toward Death: From the Middle Ages to the Present*. Translated by Patricia M. Ranum. Johns Hopkins Symposia in Comparative History 4. Baltimore: Johns Hopkins University Press, 1974.

Augustine. *Confessions*. Translated by William Watts. 2 vols. Loeb Classical Library. Cambridge: Harvard University Press, 1946.

———. *De Trinitate*. Translated by Edmund Hill. Edited by John E. Rotelle. The Works of Saint Augustine: A Translation for the 21st Century 5. New York: New City, 1998.

Austin, J. L. *How to Do Things with Words*. 2d edition. Edited by J. O. Urmson and Mirina Sbisá. Cambridge: Harvard University Press, 1975.

Balthasar, Hans Urs von. *A Theology of History*. San Francisco: Ignatius, 1994.

———. *The Theology of Karl Barth: Exposition and Interpretation*. Translated by Edward T. Oakes. San Francisco: Ignatius, 1992.

Barth, Karl. *Church Dogmatics*. Volumes 1–4. Translated by G. W Bromiley et al. Edinburgh: T. & T. Clark, 1956–1975.

———. *Dogmatics in Outline*. Translated by G. T. Thomson. Harper Torchbooks TB 56. New York: Harper and Row, 1959.

Bauerschmidt, Frederick Christian. "The Word Made Speculative? John Milbank's Christological Poetics." *Modern Theology* 15 (1999) 417–32.

Black, Max. *Models and Metaphors: Studies in Language and Philosophy*. Ithaca, NY: Cornell University Press, 1962.

Botwinick, Aryeh, and William E. Connolly, editors. *Democracy and Vision: Sheldon Wolin and the Vicissitudes of the Political*. Princeton: Princeton University Press, 2001.

Bulgakov, Sergius. *The Holy Grail and the Eucharist*. Translated and edited by Boris Jakim. Esalen-Lindisfarne Library of Russian Philosophy. Hudson, NY: Lindisfarne, 1997.

Carter, Craig A. *The Politics of the Cross: The Theology and Social Ethics of John Howard Yoder.* Grand Rapids: Brazos, 2001.

Cartwright, Michael G. "Radical Reform, Radical Catholicity: John Howard Yoder's Vision of the Faithful Church." Introduction to *The Royal Priesthood: Essays Ecclesiological and Ecumenical*, by John Howard Yoder. Edited by Michael G. Cartwright, 1–52. Scottdale, PA: Herald, 1998.

Coles, Romand. "The Wild Patience of John Howard Yoder: 'Outsiders' and the 'Otherness of the Church.'" *Modern Theology* 18 (2002) 305–31.

Connolly, William E. "Politics and Vision." In *Democracy and Vision: Sheldon Wolin and the Vicissitudes of the Political*, edited by Aryeh Botwinick and William E. Connolly, 3–24. Princeton: Princeton University Press, 2001.

Crisp, Oliver D. "Robert Jenson on the Pre-existence of Christ." *Modern Theology* 23 (2007) 27–45.

Davies, Brian. *The Thought of Thomas Aquinas*. Oxford: Clarendon, 1992.

Dorrien, Gary J. *Soul in Society: The Making and Renewal of Social Christianity*. Minneapolis: Fortress, 1995.

Fogelin, Robert J. "Wittgenstein's Critique of Philosophy." In *The Cambridge Companion to Wittgenstein*, edited by Hans Sluga and David G. Stern, 34–58. Cambridge: Cambridge University Press, 1996.

Gunton, Colin, editor. *The Cambridge Companion to Christian Doctrine*. Cambridge Companions to Religion. Cambridge: Cambridge University Press, 1997.

———. "The Doctrine of Creation." In *The Cambridge Companion to Christian Doctrine*, edited by Colin Gunton, 141–57. Cambridge Companions to Religion. Cambridge: Cambridge University Press, 1997.

Grisez, Germain G. "The First Principle of Practical Reason." In *Aquinas: A Collection of Critical Essays*, edited by Anthony Kenny, 340–82. Garden City: Anchor, 1969.

Harink, Douglas. "For or Against the Nations: Yoder and Hauerwas, What's the Difference?" *Toronto Journal of Theology* 17 (2001) 167–85.

Hart, David Bentley. *The Beauty of the Infinite: The Aesthetics of Christian Truth*. Grand Rapids: Eerdmans, 2003.

Hauerwas, Stanley. *After Christendom? How the Church Is to Behave If Freedom, Justice, and a Christian Nation Are Bad Ideas*. Nashville: Abingdon, 1991.

———. *A Better Hope: Resources for a Church Confronting Capitalism, Democracy, and Postmodernity*. Grand Rapids: Brazos, 2000.

———. "Failure of Communication or A Case of Uncomprehending Feminism." *Scottish Journal of Theology* 50 (1997) 228–39.

———. *The Peaceable Kingdom: A Primer in Christian Ethics*. Notre Dame: University of Notre Dame Press, 1983.

———. *Performing the Faith: Bonhoeffer and the Practice of Nonviolence*. Grand Rapids: Brazos, 2004.

———. Foreword to *The Politics of the Cross: The Theology and Social Ethics of John Howard Yoder*, by Craig A. Carter, 9–12. Grand Rapids: Brazos, 2001.

———. "Messianic Pacifism." *Worldview* 16, no. 6 (June 1973) 23–33.

———. *Sanctify Them in the Truth: Holiness Exemplified*. Nashville: Abingdon, 1998.

———. *Truthfulness and Tragedy*. Notre Dame: University of Notre Dame Press, 1977.
———. *Unleashing the Scripture: Freeing the Bible from Captivity to America*. Nashville: Abingdon, 1993.
———. *Wilderness Wanderings: Probing Twentieth-Century Theology and Philosophy*. Boulder: Westview, 1997.
———. *With the Grain of the Universe: The Church's Witness and Natural Theology*. Grand Rapids: Brazos, 2001.
———, and L. Gregory Jones, editors. *Why Narrative? Readings in Narrative Theology*. Reprint, Eugene, OR: Wipf and Stock, 1997.
———, Nancey Murphy, and Mark Nation, editors. *Theology Without Foundations: Religious Practice and the Future of Theological Truth*. Nashville: Abingdon, 1994.
———, and Samuel Wells, editors. *The Blackwell Companion to Christian Ethics*. Blackwell Companions to Religion. Oxford: Blackwell, 2004.
———, and William H. Willimon. *Resident Aliens: Life in the Christian Colony*. Nashville: Abingdon, 1989.
Hunsinger, George. *Disruptive Grace: Studies in the Theology of Karl Barth*. Grand Rapids: Eerdmans, 2000.
Jenson, Robert W. "The Church and the Sacraments." In *The Cambridge Companion to Christian Doctrine*, edited by Colin Gunton, 207–25. Cambridge Companions to Religion. Cambridge: Cambridge University Press, 1997.
———. *Systematic Theology*. Vol. 1, *The Triune God*. Oxford: Oxford University Press, 1997.
———. *Systematic Theology*. Vol. 2, *The Works of God*. Oxford: Oxford University Press, 1999.
Jordan, Mark. "Theology and Philosophy." In *The Cambridge Companion to Aquinas*, edited by Norman Kretzmann and Eleonore Stump, 232–51. New York: Cambridge University Press: 1993.
Kallenberg, Brad J. *Ethics as Grammar: Changing the Postmodern Subject*. Notre Dame: University of Notre Dame Press, 2001.
Kenny, Anthony, editor. *Aquinas: A Collection of Critical Essays*. Garden City: Anchor, 1969.
Kerr, Fergus. *After Aquinas: Versions of Thomism*. Oxford: Blackwell, 2002.
———. *Theology after Wittgenstein*. 2nd ed. London: SPCK, 1997.
Koontz, Gayle Gerber. "Confessional Theology in a Pluralistic Context: A Study of the Theology Ethics of H. Richard Niebuhr and John H. Yoder." PhD diss., Boston University, 1985.
Kreider, Alan. "Christ, Culture, and Truth-telling." *The Conrad Grebel Review* 15 (1997) 207–33.
Kretzmann, Norman, and Eleonore Stump, editors. *The Cambridge Companion to Aquinas*. Cambridge: Cambridge University Press: 1993.
———. "Introduction." In *The Cambridge Companion to Aquinas*, edited by Norman Kretzmann and Eleonore Stump, 1–11. Cambridge: Cambridge University Press, 1993.

Kuhn, Thomas. *The Structure of Scientific Revolutions*. Chicago: University of Chicago Press, 1962.

Kurosawa, Akira, director, and Donald Richie, editor. *Rashomon*. Rutgers Films in Print 6. New Brunswick, NJ: Rutgers University Press, 1987.

Lakoff, George. *Moral Politics: What Conservatives Know that Liberals Don't*. Chicago: University of Chicago Press, 1996.

Lakoff, George, and Mark Johnson. *Metaphors We Live By*. Chicago: University of Chicago Press, 1980.

———. *Philosophy in the Flesh: The Embodied Mind and Its Challenge to Western Thought*. New York: Basic Books, 1999.

Lewis, Bernard. "The Revolt of Islam." *The New Yorker*, November 19, 2001.

Lindbeck, George. *The Nature of Doctrine: Religion and Theology in a Postliberal Age*. Philadelphia: Westminster, 1984.

Littell, Franklin H. *The Anabaptist View of the Church: A Study in the Origins of Sectarian Protestantism*. Boston: Starr King, 1958.

MacIntyre, Alasdair. *After Virtue: A Study in Moral Theory*. 2d edition. Notre Dame: University of Notre Dame Press, 1984.

———. *Dependent Rational Animals: Why Human Beings Need the Virtues*. Chicago: Open Court, 1999.

———. "Epistemological Crises, Dramatic Narrative, and the Philosophy of Science." In *Why Narrative?* edited by Stanley Hauerwas and L. Gregory Jones, 138–57. Reprint, Eugene, OR: Wipf and Stock, 1997.

———. *Three Rival Versions of Moral Enquiry: Encyclopedia, Genealogy, and Tradition*. Notre Dame: University of Notre Dame Press, 1990.

———. *Whose Justice? Which Rationality?* Notre Dame: University of Notre Dame Press, 1984.

Mathison, Keith A. *Given for You: Reclaiming Calvin's Doctrine of the Lord's Supper*. Phillipsburg, NJ: P & R, 2002.

May, William F. *The Physician's Covenant: Images of the Healer in Medical Ethics*. Philadelphia: Westminster, 1983.

McClendon, James. *Systematic Theology*. Vol. 1, *Ethics*. Nashville: Abingdon, 1986.

———. Review of *Christian Existence Today*, by Stanley Hauerwas. *Theology Today* 46 (1990) 425–27.

McFague, Sallie. *Models of God: Theology for an Ecological, Nuclear Age*. Philadelphia: Fortress, 1987.

Milbank, John. "Intensities." *Modern Theology* 15 (1999) 445–97.

———. *Theology and Social Theory: Beyond Secular Reason*. Oxford: Blackwell, 1990.

———. *The Word Made Strange: Theology, Language, Culture*. Oxford: Blackwell, 1997.

Milbank, John, and Catherine Pickstock. *Truth in Aquinas*. London: Routledge, 2001.

Milbank, John, Catherine Pickstock, and Graham Ward, editors. *Radical Orthodoxy: A New Theology*. London: Routledge, 1999.

———. "Suspending the Material: The Turn of Radical Orthodoxy." In *Radical Orthodoxy: A New Theology*, edited by John Milbank, Catherine Pickstock, and Graham Ward, 1–20. London: Routledge, 1999.
Monk, Ray. *Ludwig Wittgenstein: The Duty of Genius*. London: Vintage, 1991.
Ogden, C. K., and I. A. Richards. *The Meaning of Meaning: A Study of the Influence of Language upon Thought and of the Science of Symbolism*. New York: Harcourt Brace, 1930.
Pickstock, Catherine. *After Writing: On the Liturgical Consummation of Philosophy*. Oxford: Blackwell, 1997.
Pinches, Charles R. *Theology and Action: After Theory in Christian Ethics*. Grand Rapids: Eerdmans, 2002.
Pipkin, H. Wayne, and John H. Yoder, editors. *Balthasar Hubmaier: Theologian of Anabaptism*. Classics of the Radical Reformation 5. Scottdale, PA: Herald, 1989.
Polkinghorne, John. *The Faith of a Physicist*. Gifford Lectures. Princeton: Princeton University Press, 1994.
Reames, Kent. "Why Yoder Is Not Hauerwas and Why It Matters." Paper presented at the Society of Christian Ethics annual meeting, San Francisco, CA, January 1999
Rempel, John D. *The Lord's Supper in Anabaptism*. Scottdale, PA: Herald, 1993.
Richards, I. A. *The Philosophy of Rhetoric*. New York: Oxford University Press, 1936.
Rogers, Eugene F., Jr. *Thomas Aquinas and Karl Barth: Sacred Doctrine and the Natural Knowledge of God*. Revisions. Notre Dame: University of Notre Dame Press, 1995.
Schillebeeckx, Edward. *The Eucharist*. New York: Burns & Oates, 2005.
Shuman, Joel James. *The Body of Compassion: Ethics, Medicine, and the Church*. Radical Traditions. Boulder: Westview, 1999.
Sluga, Hans, and David G. Stern, editors. *The Cambridge Companion to Wittgenstein*. Cambridge: Cambridge University Press, 1996.
Sontag, Susan. *Illness as Metaphor; and, AIDS and Its Metaphors*. 1st Anchor Books edition. New York: Doubleday, 1990.
Soskice, Janet Martin. *Metaphor and Religious Language*. New York: Oxford University Press, 1985.
Stout, Jeffrey. *Democracy and Tradition*. New Forum Books. Princeton: Princeton University Press, 2003.
———. *Ethics after Babel: The Languages of Morals and Their Discontents*. Revised edition. Princeton: Princeton University Press, 2001.
Thatcher, Tom. "Empty Metaphors and Apocalyptic Rhetoric." *Journal of the American Academy of Religion* 66 (1998) 549–70.
Toulmin, Stephen. *Cosmopolis: The Hidden Agenda of Modernity*. Chicago: University of Chicago Press, 1992.
Virilio, Paul. *The Original Accident*. Cambridge: Polity, 2007.
Walzer, Michael. *Thick and Thin: Moral Argument at Home and Abroad*. Notre Dame: University of Notre Dame Press, 1994.
Weaver, Alain Epp. "After Politics: John Howard Yoder, Body Politics, and the Witnessing Church." *The Review of Politics* 16 (1999) 637–73.
Weingarten, Hans, director. *Die Fetten Jahre sind vorbei*. Berlin: Y3 Film, 2004.

Westberg, Daniel. *Right Practical Reason: Aristotle, Action, and Prudence in Aquinas.* Oxford Theological Monographs. Oxford: Clarendon, 1994.
Wilken, Robert Louis. *The Spirit of Early Christian Thought: Seeking the Face of God.* New Haven: Yale University Press, 2003.
Williams, George H., and Angel Mergal, editors. *Spiritual and Anabaptist Writers.* Library of Christian Classics 25. Philadelphia: Westminster, 1957.
Williams, Rowan. *On Christian Theology.* Oxford: Blackwell, 2000.
Wittgenstein, Ludwig. *Philosophical Investigations.* Translated by G. E. M. Anscombe. New York: Macmillan, 1953.
———. *Tractatus Logico Philosophicus.* Translated by D. F. Pears and B. F. McGuinness. London: Routledge, 2001.
Wolin, Sheldon. *Politics and Vision.* Revised edition. Princeton: Princeton University Press, 2004.
Yoder, John Howard. *Body Politics: Five Practices of the Christian Community before the Watching World.* Scottdale, PA: Herald, 2001.
———. *The Christian Witness to the State.* Reprint, Eugene, OR: Wipf & Stock, 1997.
———. *For the Nations: Essays Public and Evangelical.* Grand Rapids: Eerdmans, 1997.
———. "Meaning after Babble." *Journal of Religious Ethics* 24 (1996) 125–38.
———. *Nevertheless: The Varieties and Shortcomings of Religious Pacifism.* Revised edition. Scottdale, PA: Herald, 1992.
———. *The Original Revolution.* Scottdale, PA: Herald, 1971.
———. *Preface to Theology: Christology and Theological Method.* Edited by Stanley Hauerwas and J. Alexander Sider. Grand Rapids: Brazos, 2002.
———. *The Priestly Kingdom: Social Ethics as Gospel.* Notre Dame: University of Notre Dame Press, 1984.
———. *The Royal Priesthood: Essays Ecclesiological and Ecumenical.* Edited by Michael G. Cartwright. Scottdale, PA: Herald, 1998.
———. "Sacrament as Social Process." *Theology Today* 48 (1991) 33–44.
———. "Walk and Word: The Alternatives to Methodologism." In *Theology Without Foundations: Religious Practice and the Future of Theological Truth.* Edited by Stanley Hauerwas, Nancey Murphy, and Mark Nation, 77–90. Nashville: Abingdon, 1994.
Zorn, Hans. "Grammar, Doctrines, and Practice." *Journal of Religion* 75 (1995) 509–20.

# INDEX

Abraham, 62, 124
Adam (as type of Christ), 107–8
Adams, Nicholas, 83n48, 85n6
adoption, 101, 113–14
adoration, xix
agape, 30
AIDS, 56, 59, 63
America, xvii, xxi, 29, 41–44, 124–28, 132, 134
Anabaptism, xvii, 6, 66–67, 72–83
analogy, 89–90
anger, 95n34
Arendt, Hannah, 4
Aristotle, 52, 52n9, 54, 56, 58, 70n15, 75n31, 84, 85n3, 87, 92, 94, 95n34, 96
ascension, xviii, 74, 74n27, 79
Ashworth, Justin, 35n58
Augustine, xix, 50, 52, 54, 67–69, 92, 96, 112–13
authenticity, 22, 71, 71n17
authority, 97, 133
   moral, 58
   of scripture, xix, 86
   of tradition, xvi
   sovereign, 5–6, 10, 15,
Averroism, 86
Ayer, A. J., 66n1

baptism, 34n53, 36, 37n65, 62–63, 74, 127, 131
Barth, Karl, xix, 38n66, 85, 100, 106–8, 111, 113
Basil of Caesarea, 103

Bauerschmidt, Frederick Christian, 91
Black, Max, 53n15
body of Christ, 65, 72, 72n23, 73, 75n28, 77, 79, 81, 109, 128, 131–32
embodiment, 49–51, 53–55, 59, 75
boldness, 20–21
Boyle, Nicholas, 27
*bricoleur/bricolage*, 88, 92–93, 95–97, 99
Bulgakov, Sergius, 74n27, 100–101
Bullinger, Heinrich, 6, 6n4
Burrell, David, 86

cancer, 47, 56–57, 59–61, 61n36, 63
capitalism, xx, 27
care, xxii, 47–49, 59–61, 63–65, 101–2, 114–15
Carter, Craig, 18
Cartwright, Michael, 31, 37n66
chaos/fate, 102, 117, 117n35
character, 6, 42
chastity, 95
choice, freedom of, 27, 123–25, 127
Christ's nature
   divine, 74, 77
   human, 74, 77, 79
Christendom, 20, 25, 28
Christian naturalism, 100
Christology, 66, 72–74, 79–80, 80n43
coercion, 10, 21, 23, 26
Coles, Romand, 21
colonialism, 21, 125

communitarian, 78, 78n39, 80, 80n43, 81, 92
complexity, 116–17, 117nn34, 35, 118–19
Connolly, William E., 23n15
conscience, 93–94, 98–99
Constantinianism, 19–20, 20n6, 21–28, 31n43
consumer/consumerism, 27, 123–25, 127
conversion, 35–36, 38
Council of Trent, 75n31
creation, xvi–xix, 17, 86, 91, 100–103, 103nn5, 6, 105–13, 113nn25, 27, 114–15, 117, 119
creeds, 76n34, 83n48, 113
cross, 23, 36, 44, 62, 78, 126, 134
cure, 60, 61n35

Davies, Brian, 90
Day, Dorothy, 42
death, 47–48, 58, 60–61, 61nn35, 36, 62–65, 127
  of Christ, xviii, 30, 126–27
democracy, 23n15, 29, 31, 39, 41–44
Descartes, René, 49, 84, 85n3, 94, 101
desire, 91–92, 94, 96, 103n6
dialectic/dialectical, 9, 39
dialogue, 22, 43
discipleship, 65–67, 82
doctrine, 66–67, 72–82, 84
Dorrien, Gary, 30n43
dualism
  particularity/universality, 22
  mind/body, 49, 80,
  church/world, 25–26, 26n23, 42
  modern/antimodern, 42
  spirit/matter, 79

ecclesiology, 72, 74, 78n39, 80, 80n43
Elijah, 124
Elisha, 124, 126–28
Emerson, Ralph Waldo, 41

empty metaphors, 57n24
Enlightenment, 23–26, 29, 66, 70n15
epistemological crisis, 35–37
epistemology, xviii, 8, 14–15, 23, 49, 54, 84–85, 90, 92, 94
Esperanto/Esperantist, 92–93, 98
essence (God's), 106, 106n9
ethics, xiii, xxi, xxii, xxiii, 32, 42, 48, 61, 67, 72–73, 78–79, 82, 86, 93, 99
Eucharist, 32, 35, 43, 66, 72–74, 74n27, 75nn28, 31, 76, 76n31, 77, 77n36, 79, 81
exodus, 107
explanation, 4–5, 8–9, 14

faith, 8, 16n18, 79–80, 102–3, 118–19
Fish, Stanley, 29n40
Fogelin, Robert, 69
form of life, 29, 50–51, 54, 61n35, 62, 70–71, 76
foundationalist/foundationalism, 25, 54
Fourth of July, 125–26, 128
freedom,
  Christian, chap. 8
  human, xvi, 10, 17, 30–31, 33, chap. 8
  of Christ/of God, 16, 16n18, 106, 117, 119
fugitive democracy, 23n15

Gandhi, M. K., 125
Garden of Eden, 108
gift, xv–xvi, xviii–xix, 15, 17, 86, 105, 107, 129–32
glory, xix, 102, 110, 114, 129–30, 132, 134
grace, xix, 85–86, 102–3, 103n4, 106, 115, 127
grammar, 69–71, 70n15, 73, 75
Grebel, Conrad, 78–79, 81–82
Gregory of Nyssa, xv

Grisez, Germain G., 91n22
Gustafson, James, 29

Harink, Douglas, 18
Hart, David Bentley, 9, 9n10
hatred, 95n34
Hauerwas, Stanley, xv, chap. 2, 39–43, 54n19, 92n27, 99n27, 103n4, 109n16
heart attack, 63
Hegel, Georg, W. F., 39, 85n3
Heidegger, Martin, 115
hermeneutics, 3, 23n15
Hershberger, Guy F., 26n23
Holy Spirit, xviii, 74, 107, 113, 129–32
hope, xvi, xix, xx, 8, 43–44, 64–65, 82, 101–2, 105, 116–17
Hubmaier, Balthasar, 72, 77n36, 79
human rights, 29–30
humility, xiii–xiv, xvii
Hunsinger, George, 38n66
hymnody, xiii

idols/idolatry, xix, 20, 103n6, 105, 107, 118
illness, xxi–xxii, 47–49, 54–56, 54n19, 58–62, 64–65
imagination, xxi, 43, 89, 91, 116
impassibility, 106
incarnation, xiv, xviii, 73–74, 100, 107–8
incommensurate/incommensurability, 25–26, 35, 37
information, 30, 73, 119
injustice, see also justice, 55
intelligent design, 117n34
Irenaeus, 111n20
Israel, 76, 107, 109, 118
Jenson, Robert, xviii, 107–9, 109nn16, 18, 111–12, 118
Jeremiah, 131–33
Jesus, 6–7, 14, 17, 21–22, 22n14, 26, 31, 33–36, 34n53, 48, 61–64, 74,

Jesus (*continued*)
76–77, 79, 100n1, 107–9, 113, 124, 126, 128, 130–31, 133
Johnson, Mark, 49, 50–52, 50n3, 51n5, 54
Jordan, Mark, 85
justice, see also injustice, xx, 28, 31n43, 55, 86, 103
justification (of knowledge), 5, 8, 15

Kallenberg, Brad, 29n40
Kant, Immanuel, 25, 49, 85n3, 92
Karlstadt, Andreas, 73, 75, 80, 80n43
Kerr, Fergus, 84–85
Kevorkian, Jack, 127
King, Martin Luther, Jr., 40
kingdom of God, 30n43, 108
knowledge, xix, 4, 8, 10–13, 15, 16n18, 56, 59, 83n48, 86, 88–91, 88n16, 94, 97–100, 103, 107, 115–19
Koontz, Gayle Gerber, 21
Kreider, Alan, 6n4
Kuhn, Thomas, 59n30
Kurosawa, Akira, 11–13

Lakoff, George, 49–52, 51n5, 52n7, 54
language games, 69–70, 71n17
law, 4–5
  eternal, 90
  natural, 85–87, 90, 92–94, 97, 99
  revealed, 85
Leo XIII, 84
Lessing's ditch, 22
Lewis, Bernard, 125n1
liberalism, 23–28, 30, 38, 38n67, 39–43
liberty, 27, 29–30, 101, 126
lies, 5, 7n7, 12–14
Lindbeck, George, xvii, 66–67, 71, 73, 75–76, 77, 78n38, 80–82
Littell, Franklin H., 78n39
liturgy/liturgical, xiii, xix, 35n57, 76n31, 110
Logos, xiv–xv, 91, 109, 112

Lord's Supper, see Eucharist
lordship (of Christ), 22, 22n14, 25, 27
love (God's), 30, 125, 130
loyalty, xiii, xvi–xvii, 10
Luther, Martin, 6, 102

MacIntyre, Alasdair, 24–25, 28, 35–36, 38–39, 41–42, 70n15, 86, 92, 96–97
Manichaeanism, 101, 112
Marcionite, 107
Marpeck, Pilgram, 79
Marshall, Bruce, 86
martyrdom, 17, 37n65, 74
Mass, 78
May, William, 47, 58, 63, 63n41
McClendon, James, 38n67, 67, 73
McFague, Sallie, 114, 114n29
meaning, 3–5, 30–31, 33, 50, 53, 57, 57n27, 68–71, 73, 75, 77, 81, 96, 99, 119, 127
medical ethics, 48
medicine, 47–48, 56, 60–61, 117n34, 120n39
Melanchthon, Philipp, 6
Mennonites, 26n23, 38, 76n31
metanarratives, 114
method
methodologism
middle axioms
Milbank, John
military metaphor of illness, 47–49, 56, 58–61, 64–65
mission/missionaries, xiii–xvii, xxi, 7–9, 20–21, 108, 130
modernity, 9, 19, 28, 42, 48, 66, 70n15, 78n38, 82–83, 91, 101
Moses, 103, 124, 133
Müntzer, Thomas, 78
Murphy, Nancey, 67n4
mystery, 117, 128

narrative, 9, 14, 24, 35–36

narrative (*continued*)
  Christian/Israelite/biblical, 65, 107–8
  ethics, 42
  theology, xviii
natural theology, 103, 107
nature
  and grace, xix, 85–88, 95–96, 100, 103
  as creation, 86, chap. 7
  human, xix,
  of Christ, see Christ's nature
  of God, xiv–xv
neo-scholasticism, 75n28
Niebuhr, Reinhold, 30n43, 43
nonpossessive, 23
nonviolence, see also violence, xxii, 26n23, 31n43, 35n56, 48–49, 61, 63–65

oaths/oath taking, 5–7, 7n7, 10
Ogden, C. K., 53–54, 54n18, 57n27
ontology, 25–26, 26n23, 51, 71–72, 78n38, 85, 90–91, 90n20, 117
openness, 21–22
Ordinary Time, ch. 9
Orwell, George, 43

participation, 3, 55, 74, 82, 89, 90, 99–100, 107, 107n10, 110
particulars/particularity, 15, 20n6, 22, 38, 40, 49, 60, 77, 79, 88–89, 91–94, 97–99, 109
patience, xiii–xvi, 110, 134
Patterson, Paige, 18n1
Paul, 63, 72n23, 101–2, 103nn5, 6, 105, 107, 109n17, 118n36, 131
Penn, William, 7n7
Pentecost, xiii, 129–32
perception, 57, 91, 94–96, 99, 105, 115
performative/nonperformative language, 68, 73, 78n38
perjury, 5–6

persecution, 72, 74, 75n31, 77
*phronesis*, 94–95
Pickstock, Catherine, 3, 88, 88n16, 89–92, 90n20, 96
Pierce, Charles, 54n18
Pinches, Charles, 88, 96–97
Plotinus, xv
pluralism, 26–28, 39–41
postmodernism/postmodernity, 3n1, 9, 14, 22, 27–28, 48–50, 65–67, 82, 88, 91, 98
practical reason/practical rationality, 36, 87, 92–94, 97–99
practice/practices, xvi–xvii, xxi, 4–6, 9–10, 20, 24, 29, 32–35, 33n53, 37, 40–41, 43, 48, 50, 62, 69, 70–73, 70n15, 75, 77n36, 79–82, 97, 99
pragmatism, 39
prayer, xiii–xiv, xvi, xix, 63, 83n48, 110
preexistence of Christ, 107, 109n18
Preller, Victor, 86
pride, 7, 130–32
private language, 80, 82
privation (of evil), 112
proclamation, xv, xviii–xix, xxii–xxiii, 7, 9–10, 14–17, 20, 22, 30, 37, 134
promise, xvii, 5–6, 15–17, 16n18, 26, 30, 104, 108–9, 109n17, 116–19, 118n36, 126, 130, 133–34
prudence/*prudentia*, 93–94, 96

Quakers, 6

Radical Orthodoxy, xviii, 3, 3n1, 9, 9n10, 90, 92n27
radical Reformation, 6, 17, 20n6
Ramsey, Frank P., 54n18
rationality, 9–10, 23–25, 49–50, 54, 97
Rawls, John, 39–40
Reagan, Nancy, xxi
Reames, Kent, 18

redemption/redeem, xiv, 30, 38, 101–2, 107–9, 113, 113n27, 118
Reformed (tradition), 74, 74n27, 77, 79
relativism, 26–28
Rempel, John, 75, 77n36, 79
responsibility, 20, 31n43
resurrection, xviii, 7, 14–16, 16n16, 23, 30, 36, 63, 65, 114, 118–19, 126, 131, 133
Richards, I.A., 53–54, 53n15, 54n18, 57–60, 57n27
Ricoeur, Paul, 9
Robertson, Pat, 43
Rogers, Eugene, 85–86
Rorty, Richard, 39
rules of language, 69–71, 73
Russell, Bertrand, 54n18, 66n1

sacrifice, 105
salvation, 7, 101–2, 126
sanctuary, 105, 119
Sattler, Michael, 79
Schillebeeckx, Edward, 75nn28, 31, 76n31
sectarianism, 28
secular/secularism, 24, 26, 28, 41–42, 116
Sermon on the Mount, 6–7
Shakespeare, William, 52, 54
Shaw, George Bernard, 132
Shuman, Joel, 61–64
Sider, Ronald, 30n43
Simons, Menno, 73, 79
simplicity (God's), 99, 117
sin, 10, 94, 107
singing, xvi, xx
slavery, 37n65, 125, 128
Socratic, 94
Sontag, Susan, 49, 55–61, 61n36
Soskice, Janet, 52n8
sovereignty (state), xviii, 5, 7, 15, 17
speech, xiii–xiv, xvi–xx, xxii–xxiii, 4–5, 7, 10, 16, 20, 29, 30, 50, 53,

speech (*continued*)
　55, 62, 102, 111–13, 111n21, 118, 130–32, 134
stoic, 106
Stout, Jeffrey, xv, 24–25, 24n18, 27, chap. 3, 88, 92–93, 95–96
suffering, 15, 23–24, 47–48, 54–55, 58–63, 65, 74n27, 77, 80, 106, 116, 124–25, 133
Swiss Brethren, 66, 75n28
synderesis, 87, 92–94, 98–99

technology, 116, 117n34
*telos*, 97, 116
Tempier, Stephen, 84
testimony, chap. 1, 133
Thatcher, Tom, 57n27
Thomas Aquinas, chap. 6, 100, 103n5, 106
Thomism, 84–86, 98–99
Toulmin, Stephen, 82
tradition(s), xvi, xxii, 23, 35–37, 39–44, 92–93, 96–98
transference, 57–58
translation/translatability, 19, 29–31, 32n46, 33–34, 34n53, 37
trust, xiv, xvi, 4, 11–12, 20, 57, 102, 105, 118–19, 134
truth telling, xix, 4–5, 10–13
truth, Lindbeck's types of, 71–72
truthfulness, 35–37, 48, 64–65, 71, 77–79, 89, 130
Turner, Denys, 99n45

uncertainty, xvii, 12, 117, 117n35
unity/disunity, xvi, xvii, 72, 77, 80–81, 127
universalism, 22, 25, 28, 38, 49, 91, 98
univocal being, 90, 117

Vatican II, xviii

violence, see also nonviolence, xvii–xviii, 7, 10–11, 20, 23, 26n23, 35, 48, 60, 64, 134
Virilio, Paul, 116
virtue, xxi–xxii, 41, 70n15, 87–88, 91–93, 95–99
voluntarism, 94, 99

Walzer, Michael, 98
war, xxi, 36, 47–48, 60–61, 65
war on terror, 43
weak/weakness, 14, 41, 94, 133–34
Weaver, Alain Epp, 29
Weingartner, Hans, xx
Westberg, Daniel, 94
Whitman, Walt, 41
Wilken, Robert Louis, xiv, 103
will, 91, 94, 96, 99
Williams, Rowan, xvn3, 114n29
witness, xiii, xv, xvii, xviii, xxi, xxiii, chap. 1, 19–23, 26–32, 34–38, 42, 64, 78–79, 112, 133
Wittgenstein, Ludwig, xvii, 29, 38, 50, 52, 54, 54n18, 67, 67n4, 68–71, 68n9, 71nn17, 19, 75, 80–82
Wolin, Sheldon, 23n15
worship, xix, 3, 30, 32, 34–35, 37, 62–63, 83n48, 103, 103n6, 105–6, 114, 117n34, 119
writing, 3–4

Yoder, John Howard, xv, chap. 2, 42, 76n34, 109, 109n16
Zwingli/Zwinglianism, 34n53, 73, 75, 75n28, 77n36, 80, 80n43

www.ingramcontent.com/pod-product-compliance
Lightning Source LLC
Chambersburg PA
CBHW030858170426
43193CB00009BA/660